*To Cherry, Matthew and Laura -*
*my reasons to have a story to tell*

# On The Beat

## Graham Cole

### with Nuala Giblin

Splendid
BOOKS

Published in 2009 by Splendid Books Limited

Written by Graham Cole with Nuala Giblin

Copyright © 2009 Splendid Books Limited

The right of Splendid Books Limited to be indentified as the Author of the work has been asserted by them in accordance with the Copyright, Designs and Patents Act 1988.

Splendid Books Limited
PO Box 813
Portsmouth
Hampshire
PO1 9EY

www.splendidbooks.co.uk

British Library Cataloguing in Publication Data is available from The British Library

ISBN: 978 0 9558916 2 5

Designed by Design Image Ltd.
www.design-image.co.uk

Printed in the UK by CPI William Clowes Beccles NR34 7TL

Every effort has been made to fulfil requirements with regard to reproducing copyright material. The writers and publisher will be glad to rectify any omissions at the earliest opportunity.

# Contents

# PROLOGUE

# The Beat Goes On

The idea of writing a book about my life had been rattling around in my head for a while but to be honest, I wasn't sure if I had a story to tell. After all, who am I but a jobbing actor, albeit one who has been fortunate enough to have been in one of the most popular shows on British television for 25 years? Would anyone be interested in what I had to say? What made my life so special it was worth putting down in words?

So initially I saw my memoirs simply as a record I could pass down to my two wonderful children and hopefully – one day – my grandchildren. But once I started delving into my own archives I was entranced by the story of an ordinary working class lad from North West London who had a dream of being an actor and somehow, against all the odds, managed to climb the slippery slope to TV stardom. My wife Cherry, who knows me better than anyone in the world, often told me to put pen to paper, reassuring me that what I had to say was worth recording. So now with my tenure on *The Bill* about to come to an end, this seemed as good a time as any to take a breather and reflect on my life so far.

And even if I do say so myself, it's been far from dull. I've set up Malcolm McDowell's traction for a scene in Stanley Kubrick's infamous film *A Clockwork Orange*, accompanied Rolf Harris on the bongos and tried to keep Jimmy Edwards off the booze. Then there was the time I drove the masters of horror, Vincent Price, Christopher Lee and Peter Cushing around town. I've been shot thanks to Eric Sykes; played Lulu's lover; enthusiastically terrorised *Doctor Who* - Tom Baker and Peter Davison respectively - while kitted out as various monsters; made a few fleeting appearances in shows like *Only Fools and Horses*, *Triangle* and *Hi-De-Hi!*; gunned down the *Blake's 7* crew in the final episode of the classic science fiction series and progressed from a humble extra, without a line or a name, to a regular cast member in one of the UK's biggest TV shows, *The Bill*. Phew!

It's been an absolute honour to have played PC Tony Stamp for more than 20 years, who, for such an everyday copper, certainly lived. He was shot, stabbed, beaten up, accused of dangerous driving, had a crush on PC Polly Page, a dalliance with Sergeant June Ackland (who also slapped him round the face for pushing his luck), bared his bottom for a bet, went undercover, saved several colleagues' lives, including PC Reg Hollis, held hostage and was even accused of being a paedophile.

I'm proud and humbled to have discovered over the past two decades that my character has garnered a huge following, not just in Britain but in many other countries across the globe. In fact, it never ceases to amaze me when I'm recognised miles from home by the most unlikely suspects. A family trip to Australia a few years ago, where *The Bill* is extremely popular, left me stunned when a Chinese tourist and her mates pestered me for a photograph. "Photo?" "Sorry?" "Photo?" this young girl kept repeating in broken English as I tried to take in the magnificent view of Sydney Harbour Bridge. It was a boiling hot day and the quayside was swarming with tourists and I just assumed she wanted me to take a picture of her and her mates. As I went to grab the camera she squealed, "No, no, no!" pointing at her companions saying, "Photo of you with them. Mr Stamp, *The Bill*?" Well you could have knocked me overboard. Here was a group of Chinese teenagers who knew who I was. I was amazed but immensely proud that PC Stamp's fame had scaled the dizzy heights of the Great Wall of China. I dined out on that story for the entire trip.

Personally, I've also managed to squeeze in getting married to the girl of my dreams, fathered two wonderful children and nearly lost my hearing. I've got up close and personal with the real police, even attending the odd drugs raid and been accused of trying it on by a lady of the night. Plus, thanks to my charity work I've been elected King Rat, the highest office in the Grand Order of the Water Rats, the entertainment industry's very own charity.

I hope by the time you've finished reading this book you know more about the real Graham Cole, the man behind PC Tony Stamp. While I'm happy to share plenty of back stage gossip and banter, please don't expect any nasty backbiting or salacious tittle tattle – that's simply not me. You'll hopefully find that Graham

Cole is a bit like Tony Stamp – loyal and decent – and while I'm happy to set the record straight where necessary, I have no old scores to settle. No, this is the story of an ordinary kid who grew up to lead an extraordinary life with plenty of ups and downs and tears and laughter along the way. Please settle back and enjoy....

# CHAPTER ONE

# Name, Rank, Serial Number

For as long as I can remember I wanted to be an actor. But exactly how a working class lad from Willesden - now residing in Harlow new town to be precise - got to tread those boards was beyond me.

As for becoming a police officer, that career path was never on the horizon. My only brush with the law was when, as kids, my mates and I would go apple scrumping from the local orchard. And it was just like a scene out of that other iconic TV police series, *Dixon of Dock Green*. PC King, a dead ringer for old George Dixon, would chase us down the road, threatening, "I'll tell your dads!" But he never did.

So if a fortune teller had looked into her crystal ball and forecast that my most famous role would be playing PC Tony Stamp in *The Bill*, the UK's longest running police drama, I'd have accused the old dear of being a con artist. And demanded my pieces of silver back.

Mine was a pretty inauspicious beginning. I was born at home at 58 Sandringham Road, Willesden, West London on 16th

March 1952 and christened Graham Coleman Smith. There was nothing unusual about giving birth at home in those days. Mum never mentioned how long she was in labour, well you didn't in those days, but apparently the midwife had to battle through three foot of snow on her bike to get there in time. I was the only son after two older daughters. Coleman was my mother Freda's maiden name; she'd insisted on its inclusion to keep her family name alive. My Dad, Victor, or Vic, worked as a clerk at Smith's Clocks and Watches in the High Street. For ages I naively thought we owned the place. Mum was a formidable woman with a great sense of humour who was very into knitting and religion. But according to the family, Mum was "bone idle." Once she got married she suddenly claimed work didn't agree with her and spent most of the time, "bad with her nerves." Even her own siblings, Auntie Cis and Uncle Gordon said she was lazy but Dad wouldn't have a word said against her. Mum wasn't particularly house proud nor was she much of a cook. Meat and two veg were about her level. But she did make exceedingly good cakes. Her coconut pyramids were to die for. Amazingly enough, once I'd left home, Mum actually did get a job in the supplies department of Harlow Hospital and managed to stay for nine years so she wasn't that lazy after all!

Mum and Dad got married in 1942, much to my maternal grandmother's annoyance. She was so incensed about her beloved son daring to leave her, even though he was 24 by then and fighting the Germans in Africa, she hid his suit hoping the wedding would be cancelled. In those austere days, the average bloke only had one good suit. But Dad simply wore his uniform. They had been courting since 1941 and when I started researching this book, I was touched when I came across some fancy cards they'd sent each other during the war, declaring their love. So that's clearly where I get it from.

I was the youngest of three, the only boy with two older sisters, Pat, who was born in 1946 and Jill in 1948 so there was quite an age gap. Pat was four years older than me and Jill, two. My arrival was somewhat unwelcome by the girls as they now had to share a bedroom. Jill in particular was miffed as unlike Pat and me, she never had any new clothes, only hand me downs.

According to my sisters, I was a tiny tearaway and the apple of my mother's eye. Once I hit Jill on the head with a hammer - yes a real one - during a game of hide and seek. When my sister went crying to Mum, she wryly replied, "You should have known better, after all, he is a boy." And that was that; I was the treasured only son and couldn't put a foot wrong.

When I was five we moved to Harlow in Essex, which was an exciting new town. Up until then, we were living on the top floor of a two up, two down terraced house with an Irish family with whom we shared an outside toilet. There was nothing unusual about that; it was how things were for the average working class family back in the post-war years. So, understandably, when Dad was offered the chance of a council house, all to ourselves, he jumped at it.

After the war, the policy was to move families out of London, to ease overcrowding and leave the slums behind. (Although I don't remember Willesden being particularly slummy.) Dad was given a choice of three new towns: Welwyn Garden City, Milton Keynes or Harlow. He chose the latter as, being in Essex, it was the nearest to London. It was a compromise on his part, as his plan to move away from Willesden had gone down like a lead balloon among his brother and four sisters and Mum's 10 siblings. Their respective parents were none too happy either. To them Harlow might as well be Outer Mongolia. If it ain't London, it don't count.

I don't remember that much about Dad's family, I think that's because they were a lot quieter than Mum's. And also once we moved away from the big smoke, we didn't see them quite as much. On Dad's side I was probably closest to Aunty Gwen, Dad's sister and Uncle Harry who lived in Greenford, Middlesex. I used to stay with them quite a lot during the school holidays. Sadly they couldn't have children of their own so having me to stay was a real treat. Well for me anyway. For some reason they thought they had to keep me busy every single moment of the day. They would think up activities like trips to museums, the seaside and the local lido that they thought I would like, when all I really wanted to do was to sit and talk to them. I have always enjoyed older people's company and love listening to the stories of their lives and experiences. I think that's what gives me the edge when playing different characters. Listening and learning at the feet of others has helped me bring a range of characters to life. It's an actor's job to make it as real as possible so that your audience either love you or hate you. That's the emotional link us actors are always after: to make you laugh or cry and to take you on a journey. That's something I've always felt strongly about anyway.

Mum's family was full of great characters, like her brother Uncle Ron who was a carpenter and made beautiful wooden toys including a garage which I still have. It's up in the loft waiting to one day be played with by my grandchildren. Laura, my daughter and I used to play with it for hours when she was little. It is a wooden masterpiece and even has a wind-up lift for the cars to be transported between each of the three floors which still works. At least Uncle Ron let me play with it. My cousin Alan, who was the son of Dad's sister Aunty Vie, had a wonderful train set but I wasn't allowed to even touch it. I had to stand in the corner and admire it from afar while he got to be the station master. I hated those days when I was packed off to spend the day with him. He was no fun. Thinking about it all my uncles had great train sets but once again I wasn't allowed to play with any of them. When I painstakingly laid out my own set at home, theirs always made mine pale into insignificance.

Mum's side of the family were all physically huge, which is where I get my height from; an impressive 6ft 2" in socks. Now, whenever I look at pictures of me with Dad, I'm astonished at just how much I towered over him. Like most of my extended family Uncle Gordon and Auntie Cis remained in Willesden and during the seventies and eighties when I was appearing in the West End, I would stay with them. But they would never come to see me in a show, believing that the theatre was, "not for the likes of us," which was a real pity. But a sad reflection of the times.

This brave new world I had moved to incorporated the market town of Harlow and several small villages in the area including Great Parndon and Little Parndon. I've since learnt that Harlow has several claims to fame. Its town centre had the first pedestrian precinct in the UK and the very first residential tower block, The Lawn, which was built in 1951 and is now, would you believe, a Grade II listed building. So Harlow has a lot to answer for.

Probably more impressive, in our celebrity-mad world, is that Victoria Beckham, along with *Casualty*'s Michael French, *Emmerdale's* Linda Lusardi, funnyman Michael Barrymore and footballer Glen Hoddle, who went to the same school as me, were all born there. So while I might not be a true Essex boy, Harlow will always be my home town.

The first thing I noticed was how quiet Harlow was compared to Willesden. There was hardly any traffic. Our new house was one of only 10 in Ash Tree Field. And I thought it was the bee's knees. A three-bedroom semi, it had a 25 foot-long lounge which was swiftly filled with a small settee, two rocking chairs and, later on, a chair for the dog, plus a dining table and six chairs, which was considered quite posh in those days. The kitchen was big enough to have a table and four chairs, a walk-in pantry and a side storeroom. The garden was a good size but never particularly well kept. As well as being domestically challenged, Mum was also far from green-fingered and Dad never really had the time. And he wasn't particularly into DIY. He used to do a bit of wallpapering but that was about it. Something I detest myself and can totally relate to.

Upstairs were three bedrooms. Once again I had my own room, much to my sisters' annoyance. There was a single bed, small writing desk and later on, a full set of drums. I used to bash the hell out of them and if anyone complained, well I couldn't hear them could I? I learnt the drums at secondary school of all places. Felix Cobson, the art teacher had an after school drumming club. He would get string and wood sent over from Africa and we would make our own drums. I had that set right up until quite recently when we moved house and there wasn't really anywhere to put it. Although I managed to sneak the cymbals and a side drum in when no one was looking.

Best of all was the bathroom which also housed the toilet. We had been used to an outside loo back in Willesden and bath time meant getting out the tin bath. So having a proper bathroom was absolute heaven.

From my bedroom window all you could see for miles and miles were green fields. There was the odd church steeple and a farmhouse or two along with a few greenhouses. It was all in stark contrast to grimy West London; Harlow's fields and woods were an unexplored paradise for a five-year-old boy, offering endless adventures. As other kids moved in to the road, I made plenty of friends, including brothers Pete and Robert Maynard and Steve Simmons. We were inseparable and formed the Ash Tree Field Gang, named after our manor.

It was a tight knit group of pals with a strictly no girls policy. And we rigidly guarded our territory against any trespassers from other roads. There was many a fight between rivals but thankfully no knives in those innocent days. Even when we played cowboys and indians, we only used sticks for guns. Funnily enough we never had toy guns despite the popularity of cowboys at the time. Not sure why, maybe they were too expensive; we certainly didn't need them. Instead we made our own bows and arrows. They were never very good but at the time, they did the job and we'd be out playing for hours on end. A vivid imagination is a wonderful thing. And anyway we sometimes had the odd real weapon to amuse ourselves with. Being the late fifties, so not that long after the war, we often found the odd helmet or bullet buried in the fields, remnants left over from the war.

We'd sit staring at the bullet for hours, usually around a campfire, imagining how many 'Jerries' it had killed. I still see a few of my old mates like Robert Kirby Maynard, who was second in command of the Ash Tree Field Gang. We're still mates and he now works for the Bible Society.

We based our gang or secret society as we liked to think of it, on Enid Blyton's Famous Five, although there were only four of us. We would set off on our bikes exploring the Essex countryside and discovering, of all things, churches. During one spiffing adventure we were inside a church when we spotted the loops at the end of the bell ropes. Being boys we couldn't resist putting our heads in the loops. Unbeknown to us, the bells were in the upright position, so it would only have taken one tug of the rope and we would be going up as the bells came down and it would have been curtains for all of us. Luckily the vicar appeared in the nick of time and put a stop to our Boys' Own games.

Harlow was a great place to grow up in and I am eternally grateful to Dad for making what must have been a very hard decision, to move so far away from his family. Everything about it was brand spanking new. Wherever you went the smell of fresh paint pervaded your nostrils and everything was polished to perfection. For most of my childhood this 'new town' was one never ending building site as shops, houses and schools sprang up, seemingly from nowhere. There was also an endless stream of visitors being shown around the town which was selling itself as some sort of modern utopia. For me the train station was the most exciting addition. It might only have had a single platform, but the line was one of the first to be electrified and could whisk you off to the dizzy heights of Hertford or to the big smoke itself, London town.

Dad was an organist at the local Methodist church and if I got bored during services, which I frequently did, I would escape to the train signal box. The signalmen were very kind and used to let me pull the lever to change the points. No worries about health and safety in those days. Steam trains were still in use back then and when a locomotive thundered past, it was a real thrill. To this day I can still clearly recall the sooty smell of the smoke.

Yet despite sometimes bunking off from church as a child, my Christian beliefs have remained an important factor in my life, probably influencing every decision I have ever made, from what job to take to which girl to marry and offering great comfort to myself and my family along the way. Losing loved ones were some of the hardest times of my life and really did test my faith. But I honestly believe that they have gone to a better place. And when my contract wasn't renewed at *The Bill*, my faith and the support of my church and family helped to keep me upbeat.

I firmly believe that Jesus is within me and is every part of my being and he influences every decision I make. And the way I choose to live my life is a reflection of what he means to me. It really matters how you treat people especially those who don't seem particularly nice on the outside. That can be a bit of a challenge. However, despite my faith, the one thing I could never do was knock at people's doors like the Jehovah's Witnesses. As a Methodist I was asked several times but despite my strong faith, it wasn't for me.

Perhaps that's partly the reason I joined the local Evangelical Church, Oakwood Chapel when I was 13. I've always been a bit of a rebel and not one for that pomp, ceremony and incense stuff. Around that time I was very religious and quite obnoxious, trying to save the world and all that and I think my piety made me quite hard to live with for about a year. Mum joined Oakwood a few years later. But I think the main reason behind her decision was because I was in the folk group.

Dad, on the other hand, was never tempted by the allure of this new church. He didn't like the unorthodox feel of it all and as his health was poor, mainly due to his lifelong smoking habit, he would stay at home with the dog while Mum and I went to church. Unfortunately for him, the Methodist church near us had been bulldozed to make way for new station offices so he didn't have anywhere to go. After I met my wife Cherry, she would keep him company. Cherry has a great faith but she and Dad got on like a house on fire and she was more than happy to stay at home and keep him company. In hindsight, I believe they grew very close thanks to these quiet chats they used to have while the rest of us were out and that was a wonderful thing. They always had a lovely relationship which almost made up for the fact that Cherry and Mum didn't gel.

Unlike Dad, I loved the pure joy of Evangelism and was deeply moved by the American preacher Billy Graham, who regularly visited the UK on one of his crusades when I was growing up in the sixties. I once went to see him at Earl's Court in London and was very moved by him. In fact, I'm not sure what came over me but I found myself going forward when he called upon the audience, and professing my faith in front of 100s of strangers. People often ask me why I do so many charity events. Well it's a promise I made to God to thank him for my gorgeous wife, wonderful family and great career. I do believe there's more to religion than simply believing; I believe you "pay back."

Having reached the grand old age of five, it was time to start school. Little Parndon was nearby and a lovely school, reassuringly little, just like its name. My abiding memory is of sitting in the classroom being read to by Mrs Booth, a gigantic lady but then when you're five, everyone and everything seems huge. I think listening to her sparked off my love of reading and words. She had a wonderful way of reading out loud which made the story come alive. She would then ask one of her pupils to read a page and it always amazed me when some of my classmates struggled. Reading came so naturally to me. As there were only two TV channels in those days, you had to rely a lot more on your imagination which could be fired up by a good book. We always had loads of books in the house, although they didn't belong to us; I went to the library all the time.

I had a happy childhood, which I know probably sounds boring. But that's how it was. And I am eternally grateful for it. We were loved and had the very best gift you can give a child; a safe, loving home. Having done a lot of work with the charity Childline, I understand how vital those early years are. There is nothing better than a stable, loving childhood. It will stand you in good stead, as mine has done, for the rest of your life. My parents both had quite strict Victorian-influenced childhoods; children were seen but not heard and they both came from large families. They had experienced first-hand the Second World War and I think they were keen for my sisters and I to have plenty of freedom. I would disappear off with my friends for hours in the fields and only come back as it got dark. Mum never came looking for me. Not even when it was time for dinner. And anyway, meal times were a bit haphazard in our house. And I wasn't too bothered. Mum used to serve up some very bland meals and she and Dad seemed to share this unhealthy obsession with rabbit which I wouldn't touch. And even worse, they would enthusiastically tuck into hearts. Yuk.

But despite their dodgy eating habits, my parents instilled in me the belief that I could do just about anything I wanted. Now

I am a very tactile person but neither Mum nor Dad was into this cuddling lark. But I knew they would always be there for me. And they were.

With two older sisters, who didn't want a younger brother cramping their style, I spent a lot of time on my own and was often lonely. It was books that proved my salvation. Enid Blyton's *Famous Five* of course, along with the *Just William* books, *Billy Bunter* and *Treasure Island*. At night I would lie in bed imagining I was on board a pirate ship, navigating across stormy seas seeking out that hidden treasure. I am sure that my desire to act initially stemmed from reading so much. I loved the escapism that books offered and that's what acting does. You can play so many different characters and live so many different lives by being an actor.

Happily, not long after we moved to Harlow, a real life companion came bounding into my life. After years of pleading, my parents finally relented and let me have a dog. With the proviso, "He's your responsibility and you must walk him every day," ringing in my ears, I welcomed Scamp to the Smith family home. He was a scruffy mongrel, a mixture of everything, so I nicknamed him Heinz because he reminded me of their famous slogan – 57 varieties. Scamp was my best friend. We went everywhere together and he became the Ash Tree Field Gang's official mascot. Once he disappeared for what seemed forever, after a train hooted its horn and he decided to chase it. I was distraught. Life without Scamp was unimaginable. Admittedly he was only gone for a couple of hours but it felt like days. After much searching, I found him, several miles away, panting and innocently looking up at me, as if nothing had happened. Scamp would live to the grand old age of 22, dying in 1974.

By then I was working away as a Redcoat at a holiday camp in Camber Sands and wasn't seeing Scamp as often as I used to. I was actually glad I wasn't there at the end. His back legs and liver had gone and that wasn't the Scamp I wanted to remember. To me he will always be eagerly bouncing around in the fields like a new born lamb.

Big school beckoned and in 1963 I started at Burnt Mill Comprehensive; a whopping four-mile walk there and back. Immediately I volunteered to be the school librarian and was in my element surrounded by books. Being Harlow, where everything was shiny and new, it was one of the very first comprehensive schools, run by the inspiring Mr Stirling who totally believed in the comprehensive system. His mantra was every child was good at something.

Burnt Mill is now a Specialist School of Performing Arts. Perhaps if it had been that type of establishment in my day, I might have done a bit better. School never interested me. I liked English and sport and that was it. I was good at those while I was rubbish at metalwork and woodwork. Being a boy I was forced to do these manly lessons but I'd far rather have done domestic science. Cooking is more useful. Tennis was a favourite using racquets bought from good old Woolies and rugby. I managed to break my nose several times and to this day it still looks slightly wonky. Football never appealed to me, even though I ran the church football team as part of our work in the community. The lads were great, so it was enjoyable from a camaraderie point of view. Years later my dislike was comprehensively confirmed after being forced to listen to Andy Paul (PC Dave Quinnan) droning on about Arsenal between shots for *The Bill*.

The teachers were strict, especially the PE master Mr Fraser. A dour Scot, he had no time for slackers. Once I was climbing up a rope and all I could hear was Fraser urging me to get a move on. "Faster, faster!" When I stopped for a breather, I suddenly felt this almighty whack on my bottom. As I looked down, I saw him wielding a slipper and preparing to strike again. His method, however un-pc, worked because I quickly scampered to the top like a rat up a drainpipe. I don't remember much about school but I do vividly recall that a certain part of my anatomy stung for several days afterwards. Years later I opened a fete at Burnt Mill and Fraser was still there but I tactfully avoided reminding him of his prowess with a slipper.

School proved an endurance test for me. I've always been a bit of a rebel and never one to follow the crowd. So being told what to do and what to think all day, every day was really hard. My school reports always began, 'He tries hard but...' so it was clear I was never destined to be an academic. I was simply average. So, knowing that no matter how hard I tried it wouldn't make much difference, I stopped trying to fit in and was considered to be 'disruptive' instead.

I spent a lot of time outside the headmaster's office waiting to be read the riot act. Or forever in detention. It was mainly for being cheeky. I thought I was funny but the teachers obviously didn't get the joke. Once, I couldn't resist playing a prank on Mr Feast, the history and maths (I hated maths) teacher, who reeked of tobacco and had vile yellow teeth. He was also very skinny so I put signs up around the school begging pupils to, "Feed Mr Feast before it's too late." I got three detentions for that. I also pinned a note to him stating: "Freedom from hunger. This could happen to you." Well, it was funny at the time.

As my schooldays lingered on, I lived for the weekends when I could lose myself at the local cinema as a member of the Saturday Club. For less than 6d (probably about two pence in new money) I could enter this magical world portrayed up on the big screen. I'd sit there captivated by the adventures of Flash Gordon as he fought Ming the Merciless or Roy Rogers and his trusty steed Trigger. These, along with a host of 'B' movies, were pretty ancient even by then. But sitting in my usual seat, in the middle of the cinema, I didn't notice the creakiness of the plots nor the mayhem caused by a bunch of noisy kids, munching sweets and armed with peashooters. I was hooked. And I knew, without a shadow of a doubt, somehow, I was going to be just like them and become an actor.

As I got older, my heroes were unashamedly noble. Who wouldn't want to be John Wayne, fighting the 'injuns' in the Wild West in films like *The Searchers*. Or Humphrey Bogart, cool as a cucumber in *The Maltese Falcon*. Director Alfred Hitchcock had me glued to my seat by masterpieces such as *Vertigo* and *Psycho*. British stars got a look in too. John Mills never let me down especially in *Ice Cold in Alex*. Nor did Jack Hawkins, heroic to the end both on and off screen. And Kenneth More, was particularly memorable as *Scott of the Antarctic*. All that English stiff upper lip was incredibly inspiring to me. And maybe influenced me, just a little, not to make too much of a fuss and just get on with it.

By now we had a television but there were only two channels and it never really excited me as much as the big screen. But through TV I did acquire a nickname at school. Zachary after Doctor Zachary Smith in the 1960s TV show *Lost in Space*.

Dad was now working at Cosa Electronics, a factory in Harlow and I'd sometimes accompany him to his office on Saturdays. I vividly remember the deafening sound of the machines. I vowed there and then I would never work in a place like that. It felt so soulless. I was close to my Dad, who was a kind man, henpecked by my mother. When he joined the St John's Ambulance, she swiftly followed to keep an eye on him. Not that he would ever have done anything. He was utterly devoted to her and his family.

Born in 1918, Dad was stationed in East Africa during the war and like so many old soldiers, rarely talked about it. He was a Major's batman and was important enough to be granted the power to commandeer any vehicle if he needed to. After the war the Major offered him a good job at the Bank of England but he turned it down, proudly declaring, "I spent five years looking after that man and to hell with it if I'm going to carry on doing it in Civvy Street." He must have been brave because he was awarded several medals which now hang proudly in my study. But again he wouldn't talk about whatever courageous deeds he had done.

Dad had a mark on his nose and after a lot of prying on my part he reluctantly explained how it had happened. He had been riding a motorbike with a sidecar, taking the Major to a meeting when an enemy plane flew overhead dropping bombs. Dad swerved expertly from side to side to avoid them both being hit when the motorbike fell into a bomb crater, so injuring his face. He said all this in a casual manner, completely playing down the drama of the event. I only wish he had spoken more about it. He loved cars and was never happier than when tinkering away under the bonnet of his Wolsey or Austin 8. He smoked all his life and died of lung cancer at the age of 69 in 1977. Which is why I don't smoke. I can still hear, as if it were yesterday, his rasping cough that would wake me up every morning, regular as clockwork.

Despite having chronic bronchitis and often fighting for the next breath, Dad never stopped smoking. I have a theory that those men who served in the Second World War witnessed such horrors and experienced such terrible times that smoking was a much needed release. In times of pressure I see fellow actors lighting up and getting such a release from that first puff. It's a ritual that gets them through a tough day.

Near the end Dad was in and out of hospital but he still went back to work; however bad he felt and whatever the weather. That strong work ethic is something I get from him. I saw him a couple of hours before he died in hospital. He had an oxygen mask on his face and was struggling to breath. I kissed him on the forehead and he told me to look after Mum. Bless him. I guess he knew that she would need a lot of looking after. I am thankful he didn't die alone but was surrounded by love and respect. It's been over 30 years now but I still miss him every single day. And as I write this, I have tears in my eyes. You can never fill that void and losing my Dad in my late 20s was particularly hard. I am just glad that I was able to tell him how much I loved him and thank him for giving me so much support, even when he disagreed with what I was doing. My Dad might have been a small man in stature but he was a giant of a man in my life.

After he died, I cleared out his locker at work and put his belongings into a small carrier bag. That carrier bag held all that was left after 30 years of hard work. And it was then that I finally broke down and cried. Sadly, he never saw me in *The Bill*, but at least Mum did. She would watch every episode and start shouting at the TV screen if anyone dared to attack PC Tony Stamp. She was also a huge fan of wrestling on the telly and would urge the legendary Jackie Pallo to "Get stuck in!"

At the age of nine I followed Dad into the St John's Ambulance. Dad would later be made a Brother of St John, the highest rank in the Order. St John's gave me a thorough knowledge of first aid which has proved extremely useful throughout my life. A few years ago I was having dinner with Cherry at The Hollywood Bowl, a local restaurant, when she noticed that a man sat behind me had started choking and was turning a distinct shade of blue. Quick as a flash, I ran over, grabbed him and did the Heimlich Manoeuvre, an abdominal thrust. It took three attempts before a piece of food shot out of his mouth. I was hailed a hero and got invited back for a free meal but I wasn't being heroic, I just knew what to do thanks to St John's.

In my youth, kitted out in full uniform and armed with my trusty first aid kit, I regularly attended local events such as fetes, football and rugby matches where I basically had the best seat in the house, right by the touchline. Duties were mainly mopping brows and proffering smelling salts if somebody fainted. But sometimes there was the odd drama. Once an escapologist was attempting to escape from a straight jacket which was suspended from a crane, when he stopped wriggling and had to be hastily rescued. Being upside down the hapless would-be escapee had passed out. He was duly embarrassed when he came round – but I guess it could have been a lot worse.

I also helped out on a milk round; having given up on a paper round as the distances between houses was too vast. During the school holidays I worked on a farm for Rod and Irene Woods in Nazing, Essex. They were a delightful couple who would feed me these huge doorstop sandwiches and homemade cakes. It was the highlight of the day. Rod was also a judge of Shire horses and an expert on cattle, especially Herefordshire bulls; giant beasts that could, if you weren't careful, flatten you in a matter of seconds. I would help with the haymaking and the lambing. And it was there that I had my first taste of driving when I was let loose with the tractor. Despite managing to take half a gate off, I fell in love with being behind the wheel. Years later my enthusiasm for driving would help me get a regular part in *The Bill*. Looking back now I realise I was very much a country boy. I think I might have made a decent farmer. Certainly early starts have never been a problem for me.

I was certainly a busy lad back then because I also found time be a Junior RSPCA leader as I love animals. Along with some school friends I started Harlow's very own Pet's Corner. My pal Pete Maynard had filled his garden shed with all sorts of animals including rabbits and guinea pigs and one day his mum had had enough and told him he had to get rid of all of them. So together with me and another friend, Monica Rose, we approached the council and amazingly they thought it was a great idea and gave us a couple of sheds to put in the town park. And from there it grew to include goats, sheep and the odd cow. And it is still there 40 years later.

Family holidays consisted of trips to Canvey Island, a seaside resort which looked good when the sun was out and not so good when it wasn't, or hiring a boat through the company Hoseasons and gently navigating up and down the Norfolk Broads. Again, it was very like being an only child as my sisters were far too sophisticated to come on family holidays by then so there was just Mum, Dad, Scamp and me and we had a whale of a time.

Being such a film fan meant the acting bug, which had lain dormant, was beginning to bite. Singing had been the first sign of any performing ability. Apparently, as a kid, I would sing at family gatherings while Dad played the piano. He was a talented pianist and tried to teach me but failed as I much preferred playing outside to being stuck indoors tinkling the ivories. It's a choice I bitterly regret today. A cheeky devil, I'd only sing at parties if I was paid a few coppers – upfront. I've been told that my party piece was the Max Bygraves hit, You're a Pink Toothbrush, I'm a Blue Toothbrush. I've sung pretty much from the day I could talk and love it. I used to walk around *The Bill* base, singing my heart out. The crews said they could hear me coming from a mile off. And the odd actor, naming no names, was known to tell me to shut up.

There wasn't a history of any members of the family being in the theatre, past or present. Both my granddads were labourers on the railways. Like most children, my first taste of the theatre was a trip to a panto. But that hadn't inspired me much as I wasn't particularly keen on the idea of men dressing up as women. Ice shows were very big during the sixties and I remember seeing Holiday on Ice at Wembley but ice skating never appealed to me either, I'm a bit too clumsy. So, no *Dancing On Ice* for me!

So to quench my thirst for performing, I started appearing in a few school plays, and was a member of a folk group, as Bob Dylan and Donovan were huge around that time. But I nearly turned my back on a life in the theatre when I was 12. I can't remember the name of the play but it was a three-hander and I was doing a scene where my character was in the bath so I was naked from the waist up. There wasn't any water in the bath so I had a pair of shorts on. As I prepared to deliver a line, a group of uninvited sixth formers abruptly barged their way in. I recognised one of them as the toughie I had thrown out of the library earlier that day for sticking chewing gum in a book and he'd thanked me by giving me a black eye. All of a sudden he shouted, "Oh look at him, he's got tits!" I was mortified and wished the stage would swallow me up. Promptly I jumped out of the bath and walked off stage and went home. Mr Norfolk the English teacher, came round to my house and tried to coax me to rejoin the production but I refused. I've always been a bit of a lump, big boned is the polite way of putting it, but when you're on the verge of puberty, comments like that are a killer. In the end another pupil, Martin Lewis, a blue eyed, blonde Adonis, took over the role. Apparently he was very good but I didn't go to see it; that would have just been too painful. I've never forgotten that embarrassing incident but it's never stopped me from taking my clothes off if a role demands it. Luckily they have been rare. I later heard that rather than pursuing an acting career, Martin became the Editor of the *Harlow Citizen* newspaper.

But despite such an embarrassing episode, my confidence gradually returned and it wasn't long before I was back on stage strutting my stuff and becoming more and more determined to become an actor.

The well-meaning Mr Norfolk also tried to encourage me to stay on at school and take A Levels and then maybe go to university and become a teacher. After all, I was the school librarian so I clearly loved books. But that little voice in the back of my head wouldn't go away. Just like Jiminy Cricket in the Disney film *Pinocchio*, it kept reminding me by playing that song, An Actor's Life for me, over and over in my head. And anyway, to me school was a waste of time. I wanted to be an actor. But I didn't have a mentor to guide me and I'd never heard of drama schools, so exactly how, was one Graham Smith, going to become a thespian?

And that's what everyone else kept asking too.

My family were horrified. Especially my Dad who thought all actors were from another world and, more importantly, "No one ever earned a decent living out of being an actor." But I was determined to prove I was serious and at the age of 15 and a half dramatically announced I wasn't taking any exams and was leaving school. Which was all well and good but I didn't have a clue what to do next. My family were furious, believing I was throwing away any chance of a decent future. Thinking he could shock me into changing my mind, Dad was adamant. "Never mind this acting lark," he told me. "If you're so determined to leave school, you'd better get yourself a sensible job."

# CHAPTER TWO

# Break a Leg

After endless discussions, I reluctantly agreed to put my acting dream on hold. Thanks to my work with the St John's Ambulance, I had a pretty impressive 'medical' CV so I decided to write to some local hospitals. I managed to get a job as a pharmacy porter at Herts and Essex Hospital in Bishop Stortford which wasn't too far away. At 15 I was too young to have contact with patients yet bizarrely it was okay for a teenager like me to handle drugs.

So on one particular day during the summer of 1967 I reported to Mr French, the formidable head porter, at 8.15am sharp. He was an old soldier who had been in the Guards during the war and ran his department like an army barracks. Smartly turned out in a black suit and matching peaked cap, he was always referred to as "Mr French," while we underlings were known only by our surname. The porters were a strict bunch so hearing your surname bellowed down the corridor became a sound to be dreaded. Yet for some reason I didn't mind. It wasn't like school; I was doing a proper job and wanted to do it well. And even better I was getting paid. In no time I was investing in flash gear and a little later on, a cool red and white Vespa scooter, along with a silver helmet, adorned with a St John's Ambulance sticker on the front. Although never a mod, I thought, as you do in your teens, that I was one cool dude. Admittedly I fell off the scooter quite a few times and on one occasion nearly became a patient myself when I was knocked off, just outside the hospital gates after a careless motorist opened her car door without looking first. Luckily I landed in the bushes.

As a pharmacy porter my job was to walk around the wards pushing the drugs trolley and delivering the prescribed medication. I was very naïve and it never occurred to me how much those drugs were worth out on the streets. It might have been the height of the swinging sixties, but for most of us, drugs and the summer of love passed us by. I don't think the permissive society ever got a hold in Essex. Not back then anyway.

When I turned 16, I was finally allowed near the patients and my prime duty became transferring them via a wheelchair from the ward to various departments. I remember the main corridor was a quarter of a mile long and from time to time we'd hold the odd illicit wheelchair race, which I'm proud to say, I nearly always won. There were no prizes for winning but the kudos among my fellow porters was enormous.

I had to wear a white coat which made me look older and more authoritative. I also wore trendy white shoes and a matching shirt and tie; such colour co-ordination was the height of fashion back then. A few years later the seventies Australian soap *Young Doctors* would make it look naff but I can assure you that the matching shirt and tie look, along with myself, were hip in those days. Somehow, just by wearing the white coat, I seemed to have adopted the air of a member of staff who had just walked out of the operating theatre. But I suppose that was the actor in me, assuming different guises even then.

Working in a hospital, it was no surprise that I soon saw my first dead body. Despite being a member of the St John's Ambulance, the nearest I'd ever come to a serious incident was when a rider fell off her horse and broke her neck. As a porter I had my own bleeper and one day mine went off, summoning me to the mortuary to collect a body. Bad enough but the mortuary was next to the psychiatric department and surrounded by trees which, when the wind blew, made these eerie sounds. The fact it was dark by now didn't help, making the whole scene reminiscent of a Hammer horror film and sending my imagination swiftly into overdrive. Slightly trembling, I knocked on the door. "Come in!" shouted a disembodied voice. On entering I was greeted by a pungent smell, along with not one but two lifeless bodies lying dead eyed on cold slabs. Undoubtedly, this place was a hotbed for spooky thoughts.

Dr Ivy May was the pathologist and bore a striking resemblance to Agatha Christie's heroine, Miss Marple when Margaret Rutherford played her. She asked me to wait and without blinking an eye, began slitting open one of the chests. I often wonder whether she initially mistook me for a junior doctor rather than a wet behind the ears porter. Or maybe she just wanted to show off her handiwork as, after pulling out the lungs, she called me over. Holding them up in the air, she pointed, "See that black infection all around the lungs? That's the cancer that killed her." I didn't flinch and being nosey, moved closer to get a better look. For a 16-year-old I had one hell of a strong stomach. But then I think I knew this wasn't some gratuitous horror film; this was real life and the doctor was doing her job. From then on, I used to regularly watch Dr May perform post mortems. I was fascinated as she neatly cut the hairline at the back of the head and pulled the skin over the chin. Then she would remove the brain, weigh it and put it in a bucket. Despite the blood and gore, I was fine and dandy. I'm not squeamish so that kind of stuff didn't bother me. But if I ever saw an operation on an eyeball I'd think "yuk" and it would turn my stomach. I really can't do eyeballs. Body parts, yes. Eyeballs, no.

Just like CSI, but without the benefits of modern science, Dr May would piece together exactly how somebody had died. I was equally intrigued and loved it when she enlisted my humble help, to solve a perplexing death. When a motorcyclist was decapitated, having crashed into a wall, Dr May was troubled. Painstakingly, she went through all the facts for, contrary to popular belief, it's rare for a head to be severed in a road accident. For example, the notorious story of the decapitation of film star Jayne Mansfield in a car accident turned out to be an urban myth. It was not her head but her blonde wig which was thrown out of the car window following the impact. I drove the doctor to the scene of the biker's accident and it was there that she had her eureka moment. "Graham, it was the visor that did it!" she shrieked in excitement. That night I drove my Vespa home exceedingly slowly.

When working out the cause of a road crash, Dr May could tell exactly where everyone was sitting, whether they were wearing their seatbelts or not and which organs had been dislodged to cause their deaths. Once there was a plane crash, as we weren't that far from Stansted Airport, and she was presented with a load of carrier bags full of body parts. The lady still managed to piece together three bodies. She was utterly amazing. But despite my strong stomach, I would refrain from the canteen's shepherd's pie, after a morning hanging out with Dr May, just in case someone was having a Sweeney Todd moment.

Understandably, mortuary workers have a warped sense of humour. This lot used to keep the milk in one of the big fridges, complete with body, and delight in asking minions such as myself to retrieve a bottle. Once I was trying to manoeuvre a rather large lady into one of the fridges and managed to get myself into a right old mess when she got stuck. I was so tangled up with the body that it appeared this poor old dear was trying to grab hold of me. Spooked, I fled as the boys dissolved into fits of laughter.

It's true what Shakespeare said: all the world really is a stage and the hospital was full of drama. So although I still wanted to be an actor, in the meantime, I was happy enough to, in Dad's words, "Make a living." So in 1970, at the age of 18, I got a job as a physiotherapy porter at the Princess Alexandra Hospital, Harlow, a sprawling relatively new infirmary (well it was Harlow after all, where everything was new, new, new) earning the princely sum of £14 and 9 shillings a week. Rummaging through my keepsakes, I came across this carefully typed up list of my daily duties:

*Open up the department*
*Check ventilation*
*Clean wax and replace (if a piece of equipment is missing)*
*Collect and return patients*
*Clean towels*
*Assistance - lifting and taking male patients to the toilet*
*Tea break – quarter of an hour*
*Lay mats out for classes*
*Disinfect the gym shoes*
*Check all wheelchairs have been returned*
*Assist orderlies with tidying up*

All pretty straightforward although I remember the worst bit was disinfecting the gym shoes which always stank. And once I did my back in after lifting a rather heavy lady who didn't like the idea of being moved. Quite a few patients were like that. Not keen on the physiotherapy sessions, they would make it as hard as possible for you to get them from the bed to the wheelchair, often ending up in a tug of war like situation between me and the obstinate patient.

As always I'd be singing as I went around the hospital. Once, one of the surgeons approached me about joining the local operetta company. But I declined; this was the seventies and I was more a

Rod Stewart and the Small Faces man than Gilbert and Sullivan. If it had been Gilbert O'Sullivan I might have been tempted.

I knew this job was only a stopgap, so there was no pressure and I thoroughly enjoyed my time working in the health service. And it turned out to be a great preparation for the acting world. You meet so many different kinds of people. I would still muck about, and, despite a complaint from a Lord and Lady Lake, I continued the illegal practice of pushing two wheelchairs simultaneously. Well it saved time didn't it? Something I pointed out to a fastidious time and motions gentleman who shadowed me round the hospital for a week while doing a study. He wasn't amused either.

Although I never wanted to be a nurse, and becoming a doctor was well out of my league, I really enjoyed listening to the surgeons talking about their work. The health service suited me and was full of caring people doing something really useful and I was proud to be a part of that. And it was fun. One year I created our very own medical Christmas tree, creatively decorated with bed pans, kidney dishes and toilet rolls. Years later matron came on to my *This Is Your Life* and revealed, "I knew it was you Smithy." That was my nickname, not particularly original. Now I associate it more with Sergeant Dale Smith in *The Bill*, played by my great mate Alex Walkinshaw.

I was a dab hand at imitating the doctors and when the nurses were being a bit slow preparing a patient for a plaster technician, I would call the ward, claiming to be doctor so and so, and demanding that this patient be ready immediately. And of course they always were. Then I would bluster in, saying the doctor was on his way and in the meantime, whisk the patient away. However, the nurses would sometimes get wise to what I was up to, and give me the odd clip around the ear with a bedpan. During that time I also became a union rep for COHSE (The Confederation of Health Service Employees). I was and still am a great supporter of our health service. It's only when you travel abroad that you realise how lucky we are to have such an institution.

From time to time there was the odd punch up especially in casualty on a Saturday night and, being a big bloke, I was sometimes roped in to help out. One guy was so drunk that he hit two ambulance staff. But when he hit a female nurse I saw red and accidentally on purpose decked him. I was summoned to see personnel who put me on report which meant a verbal warning. "Mr Smith, you simply cannot go around hitting patients no matter how provoked you might be." But sometimes it was hard to keep calm when dealing with a serious road traffic accident, while listening to patients moaning about being kept waiting for three or more hours, for a minor ailment. Ironically, when that guy sobered up he was extremely apologetic and couldn't believe what he had done.

One of the saddest wards in the hospital were the side wards that housed Tuberculosis (TB) sufferers. Patients had to be kept in isolation and one of my jobs once they'd left was to go in and seal the windows and doors. I had to wear a mask, as the fear of cross contamination was a real threat. Now, unfortunately, TB seems to have made a comeback in recent years.

During my teens the church was largely responsible for my social life. I would attend the youth club several times a week. It was all very respectable with separate nights for girls and boys and activities like darts, table football and table tennis which today seem rather tame. Wednesday was Bible studies and at weekends local folk groups would play. Thanks to my big gob I was always asked to introduce them and I think a few people got resentful of me always doing the honours. I also ran the church football team, despite my indifference to the sport, and every now and again I would help out at the soup kitchens for the homeless. I passed my driving test first time having failed my motorbike test thanks to the spare tyre falling off my Vespa's luggage rack during the test. I promptly bought a bright red Ford Anglia which I christened Annie. But despite now having wheels, my mates and I never ventured much further than deepest Hertfordshire, where we would sample the delights of some rural pubs and the odd shandy. I have never really liked bitter or Guinness. If we were feeling slightly daring, we'd order a white wine.

Every time I started to think maybe it's time to get stuck into this 'acting lark,' another opportunity would present itself. When I was offered the chance to train as a plaster technician in 1973, I jumped at it. The job is exactly what it says on the tin, wrapping up broken arms and legs in plaster and doing a bit of muscle manipulation. I liked the sound of it and with my sensible hat on thought, well it's worth having another skill under your belt to fall back on in case the acting career doesn't take off. I loved the job and it was great having my own room, which I kept immaculate. And being my own boss, to a degree, I had a radio which I kept tightly tuned to Radio One. Plastering is a messy old business so I wore white wellies but I couldn't resist wearing a white bomber jacket, just to add a sense of style to the outfit. If patients were scared, especially young children, I would sing to ease their nerves. And being ever the joker I would quote that classic line from *Carry On Up the Khyber*, "I think I'm plastered," which Joan Sims drunkenly utters after being covered in plaster from a collapsing roof. It always raised a laugh. About an average of 20 patients went through my hands every day but Mondays were the busiest as many an unlucky biker had fallen off their motorbikes over the weekend.

But patients can be funny things. One rather posh young lady, who had fallen off her horse, refused point blank to let me cut off her boots, screaming, "They cost £300." She was obviously in great pain but these boots had cost her a small fortune and no amount of pleading from the staff could make her change her mind. Insisting on a private doctor being called in to treat her, she waited an agonising three hours until he arrived. And the first thing he said? "Cut off those boots!"

One guy took my breath away. I had plastered him from head to toe, leaving him pretty incapacitated and yet all he was interested in was whether he could still have sex. "Well," I replied, "let's put it this way mate. You probably could but it won't be that comfortable for your other half when you and a few extra pounds of plaster of Paris lay on top of her." Years later one of the crew at *The Bill* told me he's been listening to a radio phone-in and a caller had rung in to say he was sure that bloke from *The Bill* had done his plaster cast.

My claim to fame during those days was setting up the traction for a scene in the film *A Clockwork Orange*. Malcolm McDowell's character Alex was in hospital with a mass of broken bones after throwing himself out of a window. Sadly I never got to meet him or the legendary director Stanley Kubrick. Nor was I able to watch any of the filming as it was a closed set so no voyeurs were welcome. But I felt proud when I recognised my handiwork up there on the big screen. The director later withdrew *A Clockwork Orange* from distribution due to its violent content, so my first brush with the world of film lay in storage until after the director's death in 1999.

I also did a spot of ambulance driving for the St John's at events where the odd emergency might occur. I'd had to do a course first to make sure my driving skills were up to scratch. In fact my Dad and I both did this and sometimes worked together on an ambulance. Today's ambulance staff are trained paramedics and I'm sure I would have found that much more challenging. Thinking about it, I would probably have enjoyed National Service especially if I was fortunate enough to get into the Medical Corps. For me the only disadvantage would have been that it was all men as I often find all-male company rather dull. I think it must be due to my distinct lack of interest in football.

Back then girls were never really on the horizon. I briefly went out with Valerie from the youth club, but despite my bravado, I was still pretty shy around girls. I once spent a few days working at the Royal Orthopaedic Hospital in Stanmore and had to stay overnight in the nurses' home. One night there was a tap on the door and I heard this female voice whispering, "Graham, are you there?" I was only a callow youth of 19 and absolutely petrified so I hid under the bed clothes, and kept very, very quiet. Later I did pluck up the courage to go out with a few student nurses from the Princess Alexandra Hospital. I took one to a party at the nurses' home, armed with a bottle of cider which I thought was very avante garde. But things didn't go as planned and later in the evening she dumped me for a doctor.

Fortunately, I finally found an outlet for my frustrated creativity by getting involved with the hospital social club, which proved my saving grace. The Princess Alexandra Hospital was still quite new and still without the odd facility. So thanks to serious fundraising and a council grant, a social club was built in the hospital grounds. But with only naff barn dances on offer, hardly anyone ever went there. Deputy head porter Don Leech and I could both see that it had enormous potential. Working in a hospital can be very stressful so if there's a club on your doorstep, you would surely be only too happy to prop up the bar. And with a spot of entertainment thrown in, it was a no brainer. Providing, of course, there was some decent activity on offer. So Don and I took it upon ourselves to liven the place up by putting on revues and cabaret shows.

We stuck up posters around the hospital seeking singers, dancers and comedians and held auditions in the canteen. We had a brilliant response and it wasn't just the doctors or nurses prepared to strut their stuff. Medical secretaries and cleaners would appear and blow you away with a hidden talent. Don was the technical genius, responsible for the staging and it was amazing what he could do with some coloured paper and a bit of glitter. And my Dad was on piano duty, accompanying the acts. As I prepared for the first show, I was excited, yet nervous, wondering if anyone would come. But the place was packed not only with family, friends and staff but patients too. From then on Don and I did three more but sadly, when we left the hospital, the shows stopped.

Glancing at some old programmes, a typical night's entertainment featured fellow porter Tommy Power singing an Irish ballad; sketches including, inevitably, impersonations of the staff; dance troupe Them Bones, and a tap dancer formerly referred to as a Mrs Harvey. I was a real Jack of all trades, being writer, director and compere, along with doing a solo singing spot. It was there that I developed my cabaret style which I use to this day. When singing a love song, I focus on one particular lady in the audience and sometimes, to lighten the mood and prevent her fella getting a little bit miffed, I stop mid song and question what some of the lyrics mean. The song If, which was a big hit for *Kojak* star Telly Savalas in the seventies, is a good example. "If a picture paints a thousand words, Then why can't I paint you?" Sorry? What, in emulsion?

I wrote to a gag company which provided jokes and sketches but the trouble was that they would send the same ones to everyone. So sometimes I wrote a few jokes myself which were truly terrible. Here's a few from the Graham Cole, or Smith, as

I was then known, hall of shame. "I never go away which is just as well as the missus is so ugly I don't really want to have to kiss her goodbye." Or, to groans all round, "I decided to watch the sheep trials; both were convicted of gross indecency." See what I mean? I wasn't much good at telling jokes either as I made the fatal mistake of looking at the faces of the audience, so if people weren't laughing I would lose heart. And understandably, more often than not, they weren't.

Putting on the shows had reignited the acting spark inside me. A lot of colleagues were telling me, "You should be on the stage." And they really didn't mean sweeping it. But it was a comment made by one of the medical secretaries, Mrs Rochford, who was also a member of the same church as me that really struck a chord. We were trying to decipher a doctor's writing when she suddenly said, "Why are you doing this? Surely you don't want to do this for the rest of your life? Why not use the talent God gave you?" Deep down I knew she was right. So after seven years in the health service, I'd done what Dad wanted and now it was my turn to do what I wanted.

# CHAPTER THREE

# Hi-de-Hi!

Dad was surprisingly calm when I announced I was leaving the health service and off to "seek my fortune" as an actor. I think he'd always known that this day would come and seeing my success with the hospital shows, knew it was now only a matter of time. Far more scathing was the Church whose elders virtually excommunicated me for joining such a "wicked" profession. I knew the Church had my best interests at heart and was trying to protect me but most people who comment on the industry don't know it at all. Of course there have been times when I have been offered booze, drugs and even women but that doesn't mean that you have to accept. I honestly think the Church should have known better. Why couldn't I be a Christian and an actor? After all, a member of my own church had told me to follow my heart. Yet despite their protestations, my faith, as the Church had to concede, never wavered. And nor did my belief that I was destined to be an actor.

I'd invested in a couple of books about acting and stage

make-up and started buying The Stage newspaper, the Bible of the acting profession, having spotted it by chance one day in my local WH Smith. It was jam-packed full of news about the theatre and television but I remained clueless about achieving my dream. But then I saw an advert for entertainers wanted to work as Redcoats at holiday camps. 'Do you sing? Do you play a sport? Are you a good organiser?' demanded the ad. Well I could easily answer "Yes" to all of those, so before I could think too much about it, and lose my nerve, I rang the number. It was an agency representing Maddisons holiday company. They had four camps in the UK and from what I was hearing, had nicked the Redcoat idea from Butlins. It was all very informal. The agency asked me a few questions and then said I could visit the camps and see what I thought.

So in March 1974 I did just that. In fact I visited three different companies including a couple of Maddisons, the proud home of the 'Happiest Holidays under the Sun' and opted for Camber Sands in Sussex. I'd been to the camp in St Leonards-on-Sea in East Sussex but it was far too built up for my liking, resembling a concrete prison rather than a holiday camp. There was also a Warner's camp next door to the Camber Sands Maddisons, and although it had more prestige, being far better known, I didn't warm to the entertainments manager when I had a nose around.

I felt more at home at the Camber Sands Maddisons because it was a family-run site, and had a really nice feel about the place. The camp played host to 3,000 guests, housed in a mixture of caravans and brick and wood accommodation with an enormous ballroom. And I liked the idea that as a Redcoat you did a bit of everything from organising sports to singing, even bingo calling. Plus each Redcoat was given two, 15-minute solo spots a week to do 'their bit' on stage. Now 15 minutes might not sound that long but in front of an audience it can seem like a lifetime and I relished the challenge, opting to sing. I also met the bandleader and really liked him so when I was offered a job, I didn't hesitate to say "Yes please." No one was really surprised at the Princess Alexandra when I handed in my notice. They all felt that the singing plasterer had to follow his destiny. Although I was sad to say goodbye to my friends and colleagues, and a bit anxious about what lay ahead, I was also incredibly excited. And Mum and Dad had resigned themselves so wished me the best of luck.

With my savings I bought a bright yellow 1600 GT twin cam Ford Cortina, with a black vinyl roof. It was my pride and joy. I still had that car when I started at *The Bill* in the mid-eighties. Once, when I gave Eric Richard (Sergeant Bob Cryer) a lift, he was a little startled. Not by my driving but the fact he could see the road directly under his feet. As he got out, as fast as he could, he witheringly pronounced, "Graham I think the time has come to get a new car. You really can't be seen in this old thing now that you're in *The Bill*."

Back then, when I pulled up at the camp in my flash new motor, my new colleagues thought I was a fancy cabaret act, not a humble Redcoat. One of the children's entertainers was so annoyed by a mere Redcoat having a better set of wheels than him, that he traded in his tatty old car for a model very similar to mine. Although I don't think he ever had the same amount of success with the ladies that I did, thanks to my Cortina!

Putting on that red coat for the first time, I felt I'd arrived. You couldn't help but look smart in your red jacket, white shirt and blue trousers and it did give you a sense of authority. White leather shoes finished off the look which I thought was dead classy. When I mention that I was a Redcoat, people assume I must have been at Butlins like Des O'Connor or Jimmy Tarbuck but I don't regret choosing Maddisons. It somehow felt freer and less regimented and wasn't surrounded by a fence that gave the impression of keeping people in, like I'd seen at some of the other camps. That freedom meant that I rarely had anyone breathing down my neck and could pretty much design my own timetable.

In no time I was well into the swing of things. During the day I organised the sports events, from football to tennis tournaments and snooker and darts leagues. If you were lucky, you'd find a guest who was so enthusiastic, he would organise a round robin tournament, such as snooker or darts for you, in return for a drink. I'd also organise the infamous donkey derby but somehow resisted the temptation to ride a donkey myself. I am sure I would have made a complete ass of myself by falling off.

In the evenings I could usually be found in the ballroom. Monday nights were disco nights and one of the local lads was the DJ. First off was the kids' disco and I used to dance with the little ones. I remember Carl Douglas' Kung Fu Fighting was really popular at the time, along with Y Viva Espana by Sylvia and anything by David Cassidy, The Osmonds and The Bay City

Rollers. I was more a Simon and Garfunkel and Cat Stevens man myself. Then the adults would start arriving at around 8.30pm. By then I preferred to sit with the guests and have a chat but invariably many a wife would drag me up on to the dance floor. The worst part was at the end of the night when they played Englebert Humperdink's Last Waltz and the women would make a bee line for me. As I was dancing I was convinced my life was at an end as they whispered far from sweet nothings in my ears. To this day I can't listen to that song without cringing.

Many of the wives had been left with the kids by their husbands while they'd disappear for the day doing something boring like fishing. It was as if these women had been let loose from the shackles of housewifery. I even had the odd stalker who would suddenly appear as I was going off duty. A polite but firm no usually did the trick. Some Redcoats got involved with married guests but it wasn't for me. That would have been far too complicated. Not to mention, if there was any scandal, you'd probably be fired.

On Wednesday afternoons, I would host the wrestling, which was huge in the 1970s. TV stars like my Mum's hero Jackie Pallo and Big Daddy would turn up in a battered old van and do some wonderfully choreographed wrestling. When my parents came to visit, my Mum was in her element. I had to ask her to calm down when she got overheated and started shouting at her beloved Pallo's opponent. My parents seemed to be a little proud of what I was doing, especially my Dad who really enjoyed listening to my singing. They still worried about my future, but then that's what parents do isn't it?

Wednesday nights meant the Redcoat show which we performed that evening. I loved doing those shows as we had a fantastic band and being accompanied by such talented musicians was a real honour. And of course, it was a chance to show off.

One of the children's entertainers was an ex-wrestler and again, being a burly bloke, I was forever being roped in to break up punch ups between him and some of the parents. I was never quite sure what he had done to make them so angry, other than maybe tell their kids off. I could sympathise, if that was the case, as there was nothing worse than one of those pushy mothers who couldn't understand why her little Jimmy hadn't won first prize in one of my sports tournaments.

In fact there were some spectacular punch ups during that season. On one occasion a fight kicked off in one of the bars. As more and more punters joined in, it began spreading to the other two bars and I had to call for reinforcements. Two life guards and three security men came to my aid, but it wasn't until the five lads from the band got stuck in, that we were finally able to break it up. Turned out it was all over one hothead trying it on with another one's missus.

Thursday was my day off. I recall it was a long, hot summer so I'd often spend the day lying on Camber Sands' famous sandy beach. A whopping seven miles long, it had acted as a substitute for the Sahara Desert in the film *Carry on Follow That Camel*. Luckily, I tan easily so I always had a healthy glow. I'm sure if I did *Who Do You Think You Are?* I would discover some

Mediterranean blood along the way. One of the things you always dreaded was if a child went missing which often happened on such a long beach. Fortunately, here at least they were always found safe and sound.

On Saturdays we would wave goodbye to one set of campers and welcome another. I'd keep a beady eye out for nice families that you could attach yourself to during the week. A family like that would make your life a whole lot easier and make a pleasant change from listening to campers moaning about the sink in their chalet being blocked. When I was asked, in all seriousness, "Could you come and sort it out son?" I'd have to tactfully explain that I was many things but I wasn't a plumber. But whatever or whoever you came up against, you had to keep on smiling. I'm still like it today; it never leaves you and has come in very handy many a time when 'the show must go on.'

The worst days were when it rained which of course being a British summer, it did rather a lot. Everyone would pile into the ballroom and expect to be entertained in some shape or form. We'd set up quizzes, table football, the usual stuff. Harking back to the church youth club, I used to organise a game of shuffle bottom which involved playing football on all fours, using your nose or backside to push the ball.

It was mad but it went down well and thankfully kept guests occupied. Boringly, when the rain finally stopped, while everyone bolted outside, I was always the one left behind to put all the tables and chairs back.

Again, it was fascinating doing a spot of people watching.

When the guests arrived they were often pretty uptight but by Wednesday they had started to relax. But I never quite understood why factory workers came to a holiday camp which was, after all, extremely regimented, just like their day jobs. However, they seemed to enjoy themselves. But even at a holiday camp there is a hierarchy amongst the punters. Part of the site contained a caravan park and those that owned theirs looked down at the mere mortals who had only come for a week's holiday and were staying in a chalet of all things.

A typical day as a Redcoat involved putting up the trampolines, trying not to lose your fingers in the process as they were a bit fiddly. It also meant checking the blackboard and updating it to include today's activities. And then off to organise the endless round of football matches, snooker and darts tournaments, the inter-camp It's a Knockout, along with the beauty competitions. During the day the dads were forever trying to buy you drinks but you'd have been too drunk to stand up if you accepted them all. And it became a weekly tradition to throw Smithy into the swimming pool. Having only been issued with one uniform, I had to beg, steal and borrow another as mine was never quite dry enough for the next day.

I was having a ball and knew no matter what happened next, I'd done the right thing by taking the plunge.

For me the highlight of the week was undoubtedly my solo spots. I would sing well known songs including the Streets of London and later, of course, If. Thinking about it now, Telly Savalas seems to have had some kind of barmy hold over me as during my Redcoat stint, I blatantly copied his trademark. The TV show *Kojak* was huge at the time and he had become famous for sucking lollipops. I did a deal with the camp sweetshop so he only charged me one penny per lollipop. I'd give these out as prizes not just for winning a match but for good behaviour too. And, yes, you've guessed it. The presentation of the lollipop ceremony would be brought to a close by Kojak's catchphrase, "Who Loves Ya Baby?" Well they do say imitation is the sincerest form of flattery, don't they?

Once a week big name entertainers would visit the camp and I would avidly watch their act, hoping to pick up some tips. One of these was the duo Little and Large and as I observed from the wings, I never dreamt that barely a year later I would be performing alongside them in pantomime. It's ironic that I also went on to appear in an episode of *Hi-De-Hi!* but as a drunk Liverpudlian rather than a Yellowcoat. We filmed at an actual holiday camp but it was out of season and as well as freezing cold, looked a bit worn around the edges; not a patch on Maddisons at Camber Sands, of course.

I can honestly say that I have never been so tired in my life. I could have slept anywhere. I was on duty, on and off, from 10am until midnight. I was exhausted and yet exhilarated.

And after only a few weeks at Maddisons I spotted the girl I was to marry. Cherry Ingram was only 16 and on holiday with her family when I first saw her. And like a scene from an old film, I thought, "Wow!" She was a knock-out. Beautiful with lustrous honey coloured hair, a great figure and a smile that made my heart miss a beat. As we waited to greet the new arrivals on a Saturday afternoon and, admittedly, checked them out, Cherry was head and shoulders above the rest. The Ingrams were regulars and happy to organise their own games rather than rely on a rookie Redcoat like me. So the next time I saw her, Cherry was putting together a rounders tournament that, embarrassingly, had more players than mine.

She and her younger sister, Carol, had bet each other to see who could date a Redcoat first. Cherry won when I made sure I escorted her during the camp beauty contest and decided to ask her out. She easily won the contest and was crowned Miss Camber Sands for that particular week. On Monday night, at the disco, I made my move. As a Redcoat you had to play it cool as there were strict rules about fraternising with the guests. But I was smitten and there was no way I was going to let her go. Using lack of time as an excuse, I got Cherry to ask her dad if I could take her out. I couldn't bear the thought that he might say no. But luckily he didn't.

I don't normally suffer from nerves but my insides were doing somersaults as I went to pick her up for our first date. It was my day off and I took her to see the film *Papillon* in Dover. Starring Steve McQueen and Dustin Hoffman as prisoners on Devil's Island, it was hardly a romantic movie. Fortunately, the rest of the date was a bit more like it. We sat on the beach with a bag of chips and watched the moon's reflection on the sea. And when Cherry got chilly, I put my prized green Parker around her shoulders. It must have been love! I froze, but she was worth it. She, on the other hand sat on my glasses and broke them, something she has since managed to do with alarming frequency over the years. In spite of the film choice, it did the trick and we swiftly became an item. For both of us it was clear that we had met 'the one.'

Cherry's prize for winning the beauty contest heat was another holiday for the week of the final so until her return, we wrote to each other every other day. Her mum told her: "He's a Redcoat, it's a holiday romance, forget about it." But fortunately her mum was wrong. When Cherry came back in June, she won the contest again

During this time, Cherry was a regular on the beauty queen circuit, winning titles such as Miss Penge - yes it really did exist - and Miss Personality. Whatever competition she entered, she won. The prizes varied from a set of Carmen rollers to a lava lamp and sounded more like they belonged on *The Generation Game's* conveyer belt rather than a set of glamorous trophies. She was also later a Mecca girl, working for the Miss World organiser Julia Morley, and a model for numerous fashion houses including Jaeger. Because Cherry was never afraid to say what she thought, she would be invited to sit with some of the Arab clients and tell them whether a particular dress or blouse really suited them. Goodness only knows what they thought of this cockney sparrow telling them what did and didn't suit them but she was always asked back and never shied away from giving her honest opinion. I fell head over heels for her. I think we were kindred spirits because her family disapproved of her modelling, especially when she did a modelling course, just as mine had no understanding of what on earth I was doing, seemingly mucking about as a would-be actor.

Cherry also did a spot of modelling on the catwalk but there was one time when she took a far from graceful tumble into a swimming pool. She was modelling some swimsuits and had to walk down a catwalk that had been specially built over a swimming pool. The show had been choreographed beautifully and at the end the models had to step, one by one, onto three plastic mushrooms that were placed slightly apart. Another girl had already fallen in to the water but had only got wet up to her knees but by clambering back on to one of the fake fungi, she had made it all sodden and slippery. And what's more, she never mentioned it to Cherry. So she strides along, gets to the offending mushroom and you guessed it, falls in face first, only to emerge like a drowned rat. I was sitting in the audience and have to admit I, along with the audience, was howling with laughter. I don't think Cherry has quite forgiven me.

Again, in those more innocent times things never went much further than a kiss and a cuddle. One night her dad came banging loudly on my chalet door looking for his daughter. She was supposed to have been back by 11pm but we had got slightly carried away. The look on his face was a picture when we opened the door so quickly; I think he was expecting there to be a delay while we hastily re-arranged our clothes. Cherry's dad was rightly very protective of his daughters yet he would encourage his sons to go out and sow their wild oats. Later, once Cherry and I had been together a while, me and my big gob couldn't help but say "excuse me, but these girls you're encouraging your sons to rampantly pursue are all somebody's daughter!"

I lost my virginity to Cherry. We were both virgins and our first time is a very precious memory that remains deeply private to both of us. She has always been the only woman for me. She has, in the words of Princess Diana, been my rock and helped me stay sane in this rewarding but insane profession. Cherry is my soul mate and best friend and you can't ask for better than that. And I will always be grateful for her giving me two wonderful children, Matthew and Laura.

Cherry would herself later work at rival Pontin's in 1977, when she was 19, as both a children's entertainer and a Bluecoat. She realised she wasn't really cut out for this lark when she took a group of pensioners for a two-hour walk along some coastal paths in Devon. The oldies seemed alright during their outing, managing to climb over the stiles, but when they got back her boss was hopping mad, wondering why they had been so long. Unfortunately one of the OAPs died later that night and another the next day. Unlucky or what.

My wonderful season as a Redcoat had opened up my eyes to just how many possibilities were out there. I was still only 22 and in the words of Arthur Daley, played by that eminent actor, George Cole, my world was at least a lobster if not yet an oyster. Funnily enough, when I changed my name to Graham Cole, many people were convinced I was George Cole's son or, in the case of a BBC doorman, the great man himself. I used to try to correct him, "I'm Graham Cole, not George," but eventually I gave up as he never remembered. And anyway it wasn't a bad thing being mistaken for such a versatile actor. So as the season drew to a close, I started scouring through *The Stage* looking for the next opportunity.

# CHAPTER FOUR

# An Actor's Life for Me

The letter from the entertainments manager at Maddisons apologised for not saying "Cheerio" and thanked me for doing such a great job at camp. "So much so, that I would like to invite you back for the next season. Please let me know."

But I'd already lined up my next job and this time it was actually in the theatre. I'd seen an advert in *The Stage* for vocalists to join The Bel Canto Singers who were quite famous at the time. They were a musical troupe who provided the chorus for shows such as pantos and musical revues all over the country.

I headed up to London for the audition which was being held at London's legendary Drury Lane theatre and sang my party piece 'Till There Was You, from the fifties musical *The Music Man*. It's a classic ballad that's been covered by a host of artistes including Nana Mouskouri and The Beatles. I'm lucky enough not to get too nervous before auditions, and thanks to Maddisons, my confidence had increased two-fold, but I was still a little surprised, but delighted to be told there and then that I'd got the job.

As the season wound up, I left Maddisons in October 1974 and did a bit of freelance work back in the health service before heading for the Bristol Hippodrome to start rehearsals for *Cinderella*. The leading lights were Mark Wynter, a sixties pop star whose biggest hit was Venus in Blue Jeans; comedy actress Dora Bryan and comedian Norman Vaughan. Norman had presented the TV game show *The Golden Shot* and appeared in a memorable sixties TV advertising campaign for Cadbury's Roses, which included the famous slogan, Roses Grow on You. However, considering how famous he was at the time, Norman was incredibly nervous before each and every performance. I, on the other hand, was savouring just being in such esteemed company. Everything about it was magical; it wasn't only the audience who were having a ball. Here I was, Graham Smith from Essex up on the big stage with stars I had only ever seen on the telly, playing a part in this wonderful extravaganza. How lucky was I?

And even better, Mum and Dad came to see me. They stayed for the weekend and we spent a great couple of days together. They were so proud and the way they were talking you'd think I was the star of the show. Never mind Norman and Dora, their son Graham was the main attraction. But I guess they were as thrilled as I was that I was actually a paid performer in a professional show.

As well as this gig being my first professional engagement in the theatre, it was also an introduction to the world of theatrical digs. Nearly every actor has a horror story to tell about squalid digs and ferocious landladies. Luckily my first encounter was fine, but I would soon have my own terrible tale to tell when I stayed in digs that were so cold, I had to sleep with my coat on, while the lady of the house sat, warm as toast in the front room, home to the one and only electric fire. When I mentioned the lack of central heating, the landlady simply replied, "Put another cardi on love."

Another time one room was brown, brown and brown. The walls were painted brown and the sheets were brown. Although it looked like they hadn't been changed for weeks so that might not have been their original colour. They were so icky that you had to prise them apart but when it was eleven at night and the hotels were all too expensive, you were so tired you would have slept anywhere.

I stayed in the Bristol digs for 11 weeks, paying the princely sum of £6.25 a week for board, 50p for electricity and a share of the gas bill, 15p for a pint of milk and 50p laundry. The landladies were known for counting every penny.

I didn't have an agent but was put in touch with Barrie Stacey, who also provided backing artistes for shows all over the country. From time to time he would ring me up asking, "Darling, I've had a call; now what are you up to?" A great friend of Quentin Crisp, he was very camp, very theatrical, a really lovely man and a legend within showbiz circles.

Musical theatre was my first love and through Barry I got a job playing a variety of roles including cowpoke, or ranch hand, townspeople and even Indians in the musical *Calamity Jane*. The eponymous heroine was played by Lynda Marchal, now better known as writer Lynda La Plante, creator of *Prime Suspect.* She was actually very good but I can understand her move behind the camera. Being an actor is hard enough but actresses have to deal with so much ageism later on in their careers.

I also landed a range of roles in a production of *Pygmalion*, including race goer and bystander. Gwen Taylor, who went on to star in *Heartbeat* was in it along with a very young and very nervous Brenda Blethyn who played a parlour maid.

Now that I had some experience under my belt, I applied for an Equity card. It was hardly surprising to find that there was already another Graham Smith on their books. I agonised over what to call myself. Graham Smythe? Too posh. Graham Coleman Smith? Too much of a mouthful. I finally settled on Graham Cole. It ran off the tongue and I hoped it would be memorable. Plus it still had an essence of my real name.

Determined to improve my skills, I took singing and sword fighting lessons. A decade later, my proficiency in the art of combat would secure my first appearance in *The Bill* as a non speaking policeman, trying to break-up a fight. The lessons definitely paid off.

Again thanks to Barry, I did my very first summer season in *The Rolf Harris Show* at the Winter Gardens in Bournemouth in 1975. For the purposes of the production, I was now a member of the Geoff Alderson Singers and provided vocal backing throughout the show. Rolf was obviously top of the bill and I got roped in to play the bongos on stage while he painted. Luckily I

was a bit of a drummer so gently tapped along, smiling sweetly.
But I would have said "Yes" whether I could do it or not. I
was just so happy to be a part of it all. As I tapped, I watched
fascinated, as Rolf created a masterpiece from what seemed like
a few large dollops of paint. I didn't get to know Rolf well. He
was quieter off stage than on and when lots of us in the show went
out clubbing afterwards he never came along. I've bumped into
him many times since at Water Rats events. He gave one of his
creations to Cherry. We still don't know what it is yet but it could
well be worth a small fortune today.

I also had the odd solo singing spot but I lost five minutes,
half way through the season, when the manager decided to try out
this new double act. I was a bit put out but then it was Cannon and
Ball. Having done the rounds, including my very own Maddisons
holiday camp, the duo were on the verge of making it big. They
proved a huge hit and not long afterwards began making regular
TV appearances.

Sunday nights were devoted to guest stars like Lulu, who'd
appear once a month and I was fortunate enough to have the job
of introducing them. One act I wasn't expecting to see during a
summer season in a British town was ballet superstar duo Rudolf
Nureyev and Margot Fonteyn. Everyone was so excited especially
when, providing we remained quiet, the company was allowed
to watch them rehearse in the auditorium. The couple were so
disciplined; rehearsing from 8am to about an hour before they
were due to go on. Whenever they took a break, Margot would
plunge her delicate feet into buckets of ice cold water to ease the

pain from dancing on point and prevent any swelling. I remember the hairs on the back of my neck standing on end as I watched and I felt privileged to be permitted a sneak a preview of two of the world's greatest dancers.

Also doing the rounds in those days was comic Bernie Clifton, who became a great mate; Bernie Flint and Lena Zavaroni of *Opportunity Knocks* fame; Singalongmax courtesy of Max Bygraves and singer Frank Iffield. And The Chuckle Brothers were just starting out back then. As I glance at the old programmes which I still have, it seems like another world, especially with the glossy cigarette adverts littering every other page.

At that time Cherry was doing the beauty competition circuit, so we'd often have to meet up at faceless motorway service stations up and down the country. Or, being extremely poor, in her dad's front room just like Penny and Vince in John Sullivan's classic sitcom, *Just Good Friends*. Cherry's dad couldn't half moan. I was earning the Equity bare minimum of £120 a week, hardly a fortune and most of that was going on digs. If you could find anything below £50 you were doing well. In the end I bought a caravan and Cherry used to come and stay with me at weekends. It proved an ideal solution and a real haven for us.

Originally we bought it for purely practical reasons as you could spend a fortune on digs. And sometimes if you turned up late at night all the theatrical digs were fully booked. So it made sense to have our very own mobile home. And you didn't have to keep packing and unpacking. We stayed on farms and in caravan parks. One summer season we set up camp at Robin Hood's Bay near Whitby, North Yorkshire. Overlooking the sea, the view was breathtaking. Cherry got a job in a local café and the pair of us enjoyed an idyllic summer. I firmly believe the caravan transformed our relationship. It might not have been that grand but at last Cherry had somewhere she could call home. My Mum wasn't particularly happy about us sharing a bed but Cherry's parents were a lot happier now she had somewhere slightly better than dodgy theatrical digs to stay in.

We bought the caravan from the Bates family in Sidcup, Kent. Vic was a lovely man and the van was very well equipped. He owned a car supplies shop and insisted on giving us a few extras. I think he felt sorry for us as we didn't have much. We are still in touch with them and he and his wife Irene loved *The Bill*. They were just one example of how sweet people have been to Cherry and I along the way, showing us only love and kindness.

I also squeezed in cabaret appearances at local clubs. Suitably attired in a velvet jacket and dickie bow, I was known as, 'Graham Cole, the debonair ambassador of song.' I know it sounds cheesy but it was the seventies and I was always re-booked so I must have been doing something right.

Looking back, things did seem a lot simpler in those days. I would ask around about work or write letters. An example of the sort of replies I received is the following letter from Leslie Grade's agency (Michael's dad):

*"Thank you for your letter re: panto auditions. Since you spoke to Mr Francois, arrangements for Jack and The Beanstalk*

*have been altered and another production will be going into the Palace Theatre, Manchester. However, we will be producing Babes in the Wood at the Hippodrome, Bristol for this coming Xmas season and holding auditions at 11am on Monday next, 20th October 1975 at the West End Synagogue, W1. If you are interested in appearing, perhaps you would like to come along."*

So polite. I did pop along and got a job as a member of the company, once again, playing all sorts of different characters.

Auditions are the bane of any actors' life and rarely are they pleasant experiences. Generally I would turn up at the theatre, at an allotted time and be herded into a holding area with a bunch of other actors. You'd get to know some of the faces but other than a curt "hello," wouldn't enter into conversation as these were your rivals. Telling yourself you were better than them, you'd run through your audition piece in your head and pray you weren't going to blow it.

After what seemed like an age, a stage manager with a clipboard would appear, tick your name off and guide you onto the stage. You'd hand your sheet music to the lone pianist and step, literally, into the spotlight. The dazzling light meant you could hardly see anyone in the stalls, which included the director and casting director. You'd introduce yourself and give a brief summary of what you had done. I would sing the usual, 'Till There Was You. Sometimes you would get to the end of the song and a disembodied voice would shout, "Thank you!" The worst times were when they would carry on chatting as you sang your heart out. Once, I got so fed up that I stopped and asked, "Am I disturbing you?" Unsurprisingly, I didn't get the part. Sometimes you'd be asked to sing another song or stay on and try a scene. But normally you would hear a few days later whether you had won them over or not.

Musical theatre remained close to my heart and I did a production of *Jesus Christ Superstar* playing Caiaphas, a Jewish High Priest. I got my first taste of the West End in the mid-seventies when I appeared in a revue called *Glamorous Nights* starring light operetta star John Hanson, at the New London Theatre. A heartthrob in his day, starring in shows such as *Desert Song* and *The Student Prince*, even appearing on *The Morecambe and Wise Show*, he was now in the twilight years of his career but still chasing his leading ladies and twirling around in a black cape. The producer, Alexander Bridge, who looked like Orson Welles, was renowned for putting his mother into all of his productions. A nice thought but the trouble was that she couldn't sing a note. So the rest of us would have to try really hard to stifle our giggles while sharing the stage with her. When she started strangling, My Heart's a Calling the cast would have to stop themselves from yelling, "No it's not!"

John would use so much black hair dye, covering up the grey, that the cast and crew would take bets on which drip of black sweat would reach his chin first during the gypsy fighting scenes. The winner had to time their triumphant cheer to coincide with a piece of noisy action on stage. Once, during those fight scenes, a young buck had to run towards me and then leap over my back. Unfortunately he got a bit too carried away and landed in the first row, squashing a couple of elderly John Hanson fans in the process. If only they knew about their heartthrob's nasty habit of clearing his throat by spitting in the wings. The stage manager tactfully gave him some tissues but he simply spat into them, and threw them on the floor. I was his understudy but he wasn't too keen on me as I was that much younger than him. Being the old pro that he was, I never did get the chance to play the leading role.

One of my favourite productions was a musical version of *Anne of Green Gables* based on the famous novel about a young Canadian orphan girl, growing up on a farm at the turn of the 20th century. I had to take over from an ailing actor who'd had a heart attack. I was playing the role of Matthew, who dramatically dies half way through. A few days later I received a lovely letter from a member of the audience.

*Dear Graham*

*I came to a matinee of Anne of Green Gables. Having worked with Norman, I was of course disappointed that he was ill and therefore unable to perform. However, I was anything but disappointed by your performance. I thought you played and sang the part extremely well and died beautifully.*

Considering I had to learn the role in an afternoon, I was well chuffed.

Every Christmas I would do panto and as my profile

increased, so did my billing and by 1977 my name was on the posters, just behind Freddie 'Parrot face' Davies and Julie Rogers in a production of *Cinderella* in Sunderland. And a couple of years later, I really thought I'd arrived.

As the *Harlow Observer* noted: "Actor and singer Graham Cole gets the star dressing room this Christmas after several years in pantomime. Graham, who learnt his craft in Harlow amateur concerts, has the lead in *Jack and the Beanstalk.*" Not only was I excited about being the lead, but it was, and still is, rare for a principal boy to be male rather than female.

My co-stars were becoming more impressive too. One year I played Jimmy Edwards' manservant. Now Jimmy, who had found fame in the fifties TV series *Whack-O*, liked a tipple or two and the management took me aside, saying, "One of your most important duties is to keep Mr Edwards away from the sauce." But it was hopeless especially as he had installed a huge optic of gin in his dressing room. I used to knock on his door five minutes before we were due to go on and he was already merry. He always had friends in there, including Eric Sykes. During the war, Jimmy had been a fighter pilot and I think he felt panto was rather beneath him but he needed the money. Jimmy was a larger than life character and he always had a story. As we walked from the dressing room to the wings he'd always start a story and we'd get to the wings and he'd still be telling it. Then it would be getting close to his cue to go on stage and he'd still be talking. He nearly missed many a cue. He was a lovely man, very friendly and not remotely standoffish.

He had a reputation for going off on a tangent while on stage and I really had to keep my wits about me. Once he asked me to bring on his trombone in the first half instead of the second. I could see out of the corner of my eye the stage manager frantically trying to locate it as I came off stage. As I joined in the search, a bloke in the audience started heckling so when I handed the trombone to Jimmy he blew into it and hit a note so shrill, that it went right through you. Turning to the heckler, he asked, "What note did I just play?" Of course the guy hadn't a clue. "Well, my man, it was sharp enough that you wouldn't be able to get a tram ticket in between the cheeks of my arse while I was blowing." Who knows what the kiddies made of that. But I loved working with him. He was such a character.

Over the years, I've totted up 16 pantos. One of my favourite roles is the Emperor of China in *Aladdin*. I loved belting out, If I Ruled the World, the song made famous by Harry Secombe. And I've done more than my fair share of pantomime villains. Aladdin's Abanazer is a good one and the giant's helper Fleshcreep in *Jack and the Beanstalk*. One of my tricks was to pick a girl in the audience, grab her, rush on stage and throw her to the giant who, off-stage, proceeded to gobble her up. The kids were terrified but unknown to them, it was actually one of the dancers. Unlike my old mate, the late Kevin Lloyd (DC Tosh Lines in *The Bill*), who desperately wanted to be liked, despite the fact he was playing a villain, whereas I relished being booed and hissed at by the audience.

Davy Jones from The Monkees was a funny one. I appeared

in *Cinderella* with him at the Grand Theatre Swansea in 1980 and he could be quite eccentric. He was playing Prince Charming and one night he turned up for the final scene in the ballroom dressed in a frogman's suit and flippers. Understandably, the audience didn't have a clue who it was; it just confused them. And we, the company, had no idea why he'd done it.

Along the way I've also worked with a few unknowns who went on to bigger and better things. But perhaps one of the most memorable was back in 1977. I was doing summer season in Lowestoft and one of the dancers was a 16-year-old Caroline Quentin. When you are in long running shows you are all thrown together and have to work closely learning lines, rehearsing sketches and the hours are often long and distinctly unsociable. Your colleagues become your social life and for a few weeks you are like one big extended family. And you see a bit more of your workmates - especially the girl dancers - than normal thanks to quick costume changes in the wings. It's a bit like when I worked in the health service; after a while it's just a human body. But to an outsider it can all look a bit too cosy. And I think Cherry thought Caroline and I were flirting. I liked Caroline and she was a fabulous dancer and along with another girl did a beautiful routine as a ballerina in a musical box, but there was never any more to it than that. I knew from the start that she had what it takes to make it: talent, determination and boy was she a grafter. I haven't worked with her since but would love to, just to see if she is still the same, lovely, vivacious girl.

During that summer season Cherry and I stayed with

the Wardrobe Mistress Lily Pike and her mad dog who stole everything he could and ripped it to shreds. Lily had kindly made a dress for Cherry to wear for the Miss Great Yarmouth contest which was one of the heats for the Miss England competition. Once again, Cherry won and the prize was more hair dryers and sets of Carmen rollers. At one time we could have opened a shop with all the gear Cherry won.

Much as I loved what I was doing, I decided I needed to try some serious acting, so in between panto and summer seasons, I joined a repertory company at the Belgrade Theatre in Coventry. This proved a baptism of fire but a great learning curve. We would do a different play every week. So while performing one play at night, by day you'd be rehearsing another one for the following week. Having two sets of lines in your head could be very confusing. We mainly staged Alan Ayckbourn, Neil Simon, Agatha Christie and Francis Durbridge thrillers like *Murder in the Vicarage* and *Suddenly at Home*. I also did a spot of company managing which meant ensuring the actors were on script during rehearsals, kept a record of the blocking (stage directions) and light cues and made sure the actors had their props for each scene.

Once, during a different season, we were doing J.B. Priestley's *Dangerous Corner* when an actor did his back in and I had to take over his role at short notice. We didn't have the luxury of understudies and as company manager I didn't know the part that well but we couldn't cancel as it would cost too much money. So I had to go on with the script, known as the book. The adrenalin was pumping but I thought it would be okay as we explained to the audience what was happening and after all, I had the book. Unfortunately, the prompt copy I was using hadn't been marked up properly so although I knew some of the lines had been cut, I had no idea which ones. Of course, it was only a matter of time before I missed a cue. But when an actress came downstage to help me, she couldn't find the line either and she'd been doing it for six weeks. So what hope was there for me? And because I was a company manager rather than an actor, the cast weren't very helpful, seeing me more as management rather than a fellow thespian.

The terrific Royal Shakespeare Company actor Gareth Thomas, who would later find television fame as Blake in Terry Nation's science-fiction drama *Blake's 7*, was brought in to take over the role but it took him a few days to learn the part so for three or four more performances I couldn't escape. By now I thought I had learnt the part and went on without the book. Big mistake. Half way through I dried. I apologised to the audience and my fellow actors and waited for my prompt. But even when it came, my brain couldn't compute, so I had to resort to using the book again. By now I was losing my confidence. I kept thinking how could I ever have thought of myself as a proper actor; maybe I should become a plumber. No wonder that camper mistook me for one at Maddisons.

I was so relieved when Gareth eventually took over. He and I would meet again when I played a Federation trooper in a couple of episodes of *Blake's 7*. I was in the last episode called Blake which stunned viewers because all the main characters were killed off at the end of it. Blake had disappeared by the fourth series as in real life Gareth Thomas had gone off to do other work. So the crew were led by Avon, played by Paul Darrow. In the final episode Blake reappears but because Avon thinks Blake has betrayed him and the rest of the gang he kills him. Then Blake's base, on the planet Gauda Prime, is stormed by the feared black-suited Federation troopers – and I was one of them. One by one the crew are gunned down until finally Avon raises his gun. The credits roll and then we hear Avon's gun fire followed by the sound of a load of Federation Troopers' blasters. The ending was shocking for viewers and it was great being part of it.

About a week later the stage manager took me aside. "Now that you've calmed down I can tell you that it wasn't you that dried during that performance, it was one of the other actors so that's why, when the prompt came, it didn't make any sense." If that kind soul hadn't told me, I might have turned my back on acting, once and for all.

But time is a great healer and years later that very same actor turned up at *The Bill* to play the part of the prosecuting lawyer in Stamp's court case episode, when he is accused of running down and killing a pedestrian while on duty. I never said a word but he knew that I knew and that was enough for me. And anyway, I had a former Miss Moneypenny, Samantha Bond, playing Stamp's defence lawyer.

Looking back I think that production was jinxed because a few days later I had to not once but twice evacuate the theatre in the space of a week after the fire alarms went off. The first time was a false alarm but the second was real. Five fire engines arrived and fought the blaze as the cast, crew and audience stood in the car park. It turned out that a few good luck cards, that had been placed around a mirror in one of the dressing rooms, had been too close to the bulbs and caught fire. Unsurprisingly, this practice is now banned backstage. Cards now remain firmly on the dressing table. We invited the audience to return or claim their money back. In true Dunkirk spirit nearly all of them ventured back and the performance resumed.

I was itching to get back on stage and coerced myself into bigger and better roles. But there were times when I got my lines mixed up. I was nearly always cast as a villain; it wasn't until I joined *The Bill* that I became the good guy. In one play I was the murderer yet again and it was a three-page speech involving my character making a phone call describing how, when and why he was going to commit the murder. On one particular occasion, I couldn't for the life of me remember what I was supposed to be saying so had to make it up. Luckily the stage manager had cottoned on to what was happening and took copious notes to ensure I remembered what I'd said rather than what the script had originally dictated. Therefore when I committed the murder it was done the Graham Cole way rather than the poor playwright's... Another time I was dying in my lover's arms at the end of the first act and instead of saying her character's name, I uttered the actress' real name, Daphne (Palmer). The poor lady had to spend the second half pointlessly speculating on why her beloved John had called her by another name.

Baddies always seemed to smoke in those days but because I don't I could never hold the cigarette properly. When I was appearing in the thriller *Wait until Dark*, which was made into a gripping film starring Audrey Hepburn, I looked so stupid that the stage manager put me out of my misery by substituting the cigarette for a classier cigar.

The audiences were a loyal bunch and during a matinee you would see the same double line of grey heads sitting in the first couple of rows, week after week. Once I was waiting outside the theatre for a bus when three old ladies accosted me. They had seen all three plays but much preferred it when I wasn't playing the murderer. But they couldn't understand why an actor like me was getting the bus. "Surely you should have a chauffeur driven limo?" If only. Another time, an old lady poignantly explained that she knew she was never going to meet the Queen, so, "I come to the theatre because you actors are the closest thing to royalty I am ever going to get."

My range was beginning to expand and move away from Agatha Christie, to more contemporary parts. For example, in Neil Simon's bittersweet comedy, *California Suite*, I was Marvin Michaels, the part played by Walter Mattheau in the film. My character is in his hotel room with a hooker when the phone rings to say his wife is on her way. There then ensues a farcical scene involving the lady of the night hiding in the wardrobe. Unfortunately, the wife wants to unpack immediately, so while she is in the bathroom, Marvin has to come up with a plan. I was keen to make the moment as comical as possible so came up with what I consider to be an inspired idea. In rehearsals, I asked the actress to trust me, saying that if she did, we would bring the house down. So I opened the wardrobe, flung her about six feet across the stage, threw a duvet over her and sat on the edge of the bed, just as the wife walked in. And it did bring the house down.

When I was in touring productions I'd once again be travelling the length and breadth of the country. We'd pack up on a Saturday night after the show, travel on the Sunday and arrive at a new theatre on Monday morning. Often the set had to be changed as stages can vary significantly in size. So in one theatre there might have been a door to the left but in another the door had disappeared. As Sir Michael Caine once aptly put it when describing the mysteries of acting, "Just remember not to bump into the furniture." Having missed out on drama school I sometimes struggled a little with the material, so while fellow cast members would head down the pub, I would be researching the next play at the local library.

A part I really loved was Tony in Mike Leigh's comic masterpiece, *Abigail's Party*. Tony is the former footballer who's married to the dowdy Ange and desired by the ghastly Beverley. Tony's a real misery guts and being such a naturally boisterous character, I had to concentrate hard to sustain the melancholy. They say you shouldn't look at the audience but I always do and during one performance, was perturbed to spot a group of eight people suddenly get up and leave. Surely it couldn't have been that bad? About a week letter, we got a letter apologising and explaining that recently they had all been to party where one of the guests had died of a heart attack - just like Lawrence, Beverley's husband, does in the play.

John Salthouse created the original Tony on stage and TV. He played Detective Inspector Roy Galloway in *The Bill* and when I joined the show, I was keen to share the fact that I too had played the part. I told him but he was totally nonplussed and I never raised it with him again.

My family would come and see me if I was playing somewhere local and I could never resist taking a peek at my Mum. She would only ever smile when I was on stage, the rest of the time she looked bored stiff. However, according to a press cutting I found from the *Harlow Gazette*, 'Graham Cole's fan club is led by his mother.' So I think she was proud of her wayward son. Dad, on the other hand, still believed showbusiness was full of very strange people.

# CHAPTER FIVE

# Scaring Doctor Who

*8th September 1980*

*Dear Graham,*

*Thank you for putting up with the discomfort of the latex monster costume. I appreciate that it is a tiring and often thankless task to be part of the fantasy of the costume department but for Doctor Who, it is one of the most important elements of the programme. I am grateful for all your patience and stamina during both the filming and studio work.*

*All the best,*
*Peter Grimwade,*
*Director,*
*Doctor Who*

Nowadays that letter is probably worth a few bob on eBay but back then, it was just a kind thank you for a job well done playing a Marshman in the long-running science fiction series *Doctor Who*.

By 1980, I had built up an impressive repertoire by combining theatre work with commercials and TV, firstly as an extra and then as a bit part actor. My progress was neatly summed up in the blurb which appeared in one of the theatre programmes:

*"Graham Cole started his career as a Redcoat entertainer and put his training into practice by working in rep. Graham often appears on our TV screens in commercials and shows and does some work in films when theatre roles permit. There are few people who combine theatre and film acting successfully but Graham's versatility has gained him contacts working with the greats in theatre, film and TV."*

I swear I didn't write that.

A career on the small screen had never really been at the forefront of my mind. But versatility is the name of the game and I knew TV was better paid than theatre and might lead to other things, so I started doing the odd commercial. There was one for Britvic where I was a 'featured artiste' which meant I was seen with the drink, taking a sip or two. And I appeared in a group photo for a Giro Bank advertising campaign as a smartly dressed business man. It was a nice little earner as the fee for an afternoon's work was between £100 and £200. That year I made £12,000 which was a small fortune back then. But that was only one year.

I also signed up with an agency called Central Casting which supplied extras for films and television. My sister Pat was so excited that I was now "on the telly" that when I did a play in Harlow, she was quoted in the *Harlow and Epping Star,* as saying, "*I love it when I spot Graham in adverts or as an extra in TV shows.*" Bless her. Years later she accompanied me on a gig at a theatre in Cromer, Norfolk. She couldn't get over how many people had turned up to see me and how I could, in the blink of an eye, manipulate the audience and whip them into a frenzy. It was a lovely, lovely day and I was just so glad I could share it with her.

Being an extra was a gentle introduction to the hectic world of TV. The most important thing about being a supporting artist or artiste as they are politely known in the trade, is to blend in. Don't draw attention to yourself: look natural so you don't become a distraction to the actors or viewers. In America they call them "atmosphere." The rate of pay wasn't bad and if the weather was bad, or the scene a bit mucky, you would also get paid, what they called 'wet' money or 'mud money' which would be something like an extra £20. Having been an extra, I am enormously sympathetic towards them as it can so often be a thankless task. You are well down the pecking order in just about every aspect of a day's filming, including the lunch queue. And yet, without extras, a scene would look pretty empty.

Ricky Gervais' and Stephen Merchant's brilliant comedy series *Extras* really nails the world of the supporting artist. It is very realistic.

I count myself lucky that I was able to make the transition from extra to actor, as it doesn't always happen. There are probably lots of good actors out there who are working as extras who never get that big break. Some actors don't talk to extras but I don't understand that high and mighty attitude. I've always talked to them – and why wouldn't I? I used to be one of them.

My advice to anyone working as an extra who'd like to become an actor is do an acting course and get some training behind you. Maybe join an amateur group and get some experience that way. There are loads and loads of film stars who used to be supporting artists including Brad Pitt, Bruce Willis, Brian Cox, Michael Caine, Bob Hoskins, Clint Eastwood, Sylvester Stallone, Renee Zellweger and Megan Fox and even silver screen legends from the golden age of Hollywood like John Wayne, David Niven, Noel Coward made their acting debuts as extras.

Doreen was the lady at the David Extra Agency who used to look after me. She would ring up asking the most bizarre questions. "Graham, can you swim? Have you still got brown eyes? Are you still six feet tall?" But despite her eccentricities, she kept me gainfully employed for years.

Initially my appearances in shows like *Citizen Smith* (the excellent sitcom starring Robert Lindsay and written by John Sullivan who went on to write *Only Fools and Horses*), *The Gentle Touch* and *Minder* were very much a case of blink and you'll miss me. I'd be a passer-by or security guard. But at least I was learning about this telly lark. I was given the time to watch and learn what each member of the crew's responsibilities were and how the actor can help them. Gradually my roles became a little more substantial, even if I still wasn't saying anything.

Comedian Stanley Baxter was huge in the seventies and eighties and I was in one of his sketches as a boxer. Stanley was dressed up as Barbara Woodhouse, a famous dog trainer at the time, and I was on a lead, being put through my paces, Barbara Woodhouse-style, like a dog. Oh the things I do for my art.

But I think I really came into my own doing action scenes. In *Secret Army*, the terrific BBC wartime drama that was later the inspiration for *'Allo 'Allo* I played a Nazi in one scene and then later that day or the following day I was a member of the French Resistance. When it was edited together I'd bizarrely be shooting at myself, although you wouldn't have really been able to see that.

Game for anything, I did a stint on *Top of the Pop*s. I was hired to politely but firmly push the audience out of the way of the cameras as they whizzed around trying to get the best shots of bands like The Police, Hot Chocolate, Adam and the Ants and a few punk bands like The Stranglers and The Jam that all sounded like an almighty racket to me. Thanks to my height I was usually assigned the camera on a crane which used to swoop over the heads of the audience. During the day I would attend rehearsals and be one of the stand-ins for the audience while they set up the camera shots and then the programme would be pre-recorded at the BBC Television Centre in West London that evening. The studio was tiny. There were only four or five small stages and we would have to gently herd the audience together, which was only made up of about 50 or 60 people, and guide them towards each one. The DJs I remember were Tony Blackburn, David 'Diddy'

Hamilton and Sir Jimmy Saville, who were all smashing. But I didn't have time to take in much of what was going on. I was too busy pushing.

I even did a few episodes of *Triangle*, which was a dull BBC soap opera set on a North Sea ferry of all things. It was hardly glamorous. I think the writers forgot that the weather would be grey and freezing most of the time. In one scene one of its stars, the beautiful, green-eyed Kate O'Mara, sunbathes in a bikini on the top deck and looks so cold you can almost see her goose bumps.

I was playing a junior officer and before I went off to film I was issued with the following instructions:

"The rendezvous point for all artistes travelling by train or car or coach is the Danish Seaway office at Harveston Quay, Felixstowe. Please have your boarding passes with you. If there are any problems with the policeman at the entrance, please call for Mr Hooten, Danish Seaway's Liaison Officer. Please buy your own tickets."

The budget was that tight, the BBC couldn't even afford to cover the cost of our tickets! Along with Kate O'Mara, it also starred veteran Michael Craig and Larry Lamb, who is now best known as Archie in *EastEnders*, Gavin's dad Mick in Gavin and Stacey and played Gina Gold's lover Jonathan Fox in *The Bill*. According to Wikipedia, "*Triangle* is remembered for some of the most mockable British television ever produced." In hindsight, it was probably a good thing that I didn't have any dialogue.

More up my street was *Only Fools and Horses* and I was

lucky enough to appear in a couple of episodes of John Sullivan's superb sitcom. In one, Del Boy, Rodney and Granddad were off on holiday to Benidorm and I was the Customs officer who checked their passports. In the other, Del had a dream about winning the World Cup and I played German footballer Franz Bekenbauer. I hadn't noticed the resemblance myself and I wasn't much of a footballer, but it seemed to work. And it was, after all, only a dream. What made that particular part even more exciting was the fact that we filmed the scenes out on the real Wembley Pitch. Amazing. They were only small roles but it is great to have been in Britain's favourite comedy at all.

Ironically my first speaking part was in an episode of Jimmy Perry and David Croft's classic comedy series *Hi-De-Hi!* At the audition I was asked if I played rugby and could I do a Welsh accent. Well I hadn't played rugby since my teens but I was always happy to have a go and luckily, I have a good ear for accents. So armed with an old pair of rugby boots, which I had to provide myself, I headed off to Warners Holiday Camp in Dovercourt, Essex, where *Hi-de-Hi!* was filmed. It was freezing cold as the camp could only be used out of season. This one looked decidedly drab in the winter, a far cry from the gleaming Maddisons that I was used to.

Only on arrival did I learn that the scene had been altered considerably. I was now playing one of a group of Liverpudlian lads who were in the Hawaiian bar, not on the rugby pitch. And my 'lines' consisted of egging on the entertainments manager, Jeffrey Fairbrother, played brilliantly by Simon Caddell, to down pint after pint. The gag revolved around him getting so drunk, that he couldn't let go of the bar. So us lads had to saw it off, with Jeffrey still holding on for dear life. Then, ably assisted by Yellowcoat Gladys Pugh (Ruth Madoc), we had to drag him back to his chalet, still clutching the piece of the bar.

Years later I met Jimmy Perry, who with writing partner David Croft had also created the sublime *Dad's Army*, and asked him if he remembered the scene and why he had changed it at the last minute. He explained that the reason behind re-writing it was simple. The original storyline just wasn't funny. Fair enough.

When a role in the long-running science-fiction show *Doctor Who* came along in 1980 it was just another job to me. At the time I was also signed with the Ivor Kimmel Agency. The eponymous Ivor was terribly posh and rang me one day, apologising profusely, "I'm terribly sorry to offer you this but it's a little bit of nonsense for the BBC."

That "little bit of nonsense" was, of course, *Doctor Who*. Yet today, despite my numerous TV appearances, the ones that people get the most excited about, other than *The Bill*, are my roles in *Doctor Who*. Unlike today's sleek version, with its big budgets and excellent computer generated stuff, back in the early eighties, *Doctor Who* was better known for its wobbly sets and distinctly cheap special effects. So being in an episode didn't have that much kudos. I was just grateful for the job.

My first role in the show was as a Marshman in a story called Full Circle. Back then the Doctor was played by Tom Baker, who was weird and wonderful like his character, and his assistant was Romana (Lalla Ward). In Full Circle they arrive on a planet called Alzarius, where the inhabitants are being terrorised by Marshmen. These scary, amphibious creatures live underwater and only emerge at night.

The Marshman costume was far from state of the art. It basically consisted of a frogman's suit covered in a kind of green skin with bits of rubber stuck on to give it a scaly effect. Then there were the rubber gloves plus boots, all topped off with a creepy monster mask. Being rubber it was extremely sweaty and whenever I took the gloves off, my hands were dripping with sweat. It took two to three hours to get kitted up and let's just say a lot of talcum powder had to be applied to ease getting in and out.

Like all the *Doctor Who* creatures I played, the costumes were extremely uncomfortable. There was no such thing as air circulation so being fit and void of any phobias, such as claustrophobia, was vital to the role. One actor playing a Marshman had a panic attack and all of a sudden started ripping off his mask and screaming, just before filming was about to commence. The poor soul had to be sent home.

I first met Tom Baker and Lalla Ward in a rehearsal room in Acton. At the time Tom and Lalla were madly in love; they later married, and they seemed far more preoccupied with each other than what was happening inside or even outside the Tardis. They also had their fair share of lovers' tiffs which could create a bit of an atmosphere and sometimes made things a tad awkward for the rest of us.

I had a rough idea what the costume was going to look like, but when the director asked me to make the noise of a Marshman, I thought "You're having a laugh." But he wasn't. He was deadly serious. So I did the first thing that came into my head. With a straight face I began making a slurping noise. "Excellent!" cried the director. All the other actors playing Marshmen had to follow my lead. In hindsight I probably should have patented my unique sound.

Filming began on location on July 23rd in Black Park in Fulmer in Buckinghamshire. It's a popular place for film crews as it is quite close to Pinewood Studios and it has been used for scenes in productions as diverse as *Blake's 7* and the *Harry Potter* films.

The *Doctor Who* production team picked it because it has large lake. A key scene involved a group of Marshmen emerging from the water and the one and only special effect, was dry ice creating a mist. So we waded into the water, held our breath and ducked down. The first take was a disaster as the suits kept taking in water and six far-from-scary Marshmen's bottoms would float to the top and start bobbing around. So stage weights were hastily added to weigh us down.

Next problem was that the director wanted us to all surface at the same time so told us to count to 10 and then appear. Unfortunately for him individuals tend to count at different speeds and under water we couldn't hear or see each other. So this group of Marshmen kept emerging at different times. I was now in hysterics and struggling to keep in character as a sinister alien.

Nearing the end of his tether, the director requested a Klaxon that was loud enough to be heard underwater and he finally got the shot he wanted.

My next outing as an alien from outer space was a few weeks later for a story called The Keeper of Traken. I played Melkur, a calcified statue controlled by the Doctor's nemesis, The Master. Similar to the Tardis, Melkur could time travel. This costume was even more uncomfortable than the Marshman's. Designer Amy Roberts had chosen me to play the part as I was good at keeping still, and had the suit specially made. This meant firstly, covering my face in plaster of Paris (see, I can never get away from that stuff) and leaving me for 20 minutes with two straws stuck up my nose to help me breath. The mould was used to create the mask of Melkur.

It was absolute agony to get in and out of this costume too. Consisting of a metal frame, covered in plaster of Paris, the costume was also extremely heavy. Once I got cramp in my leg and accidentally stood on a poor extra's toe. I think she was lucky I didn't break it. You had to ensure you had been to the loo before you were zipped in as there were no flaps for any comfort breaks. Watching clips now on YouTube, my walk bears a strong resemblance to Robbie the Robot from *Lost in Space* with a touch of Metal Mickey thrown in.

Once again, I could hardly see or hear anything and the poor floor manager would have to shuttle between me and the director and shout his instructions. I knew the director was screaming blue murder but the floor manager would try his best to be as diplomatic as possible. "Would you mind stepping a little to the left?" For some takes I had to stand in front of a green screen to create the illusion of Melkur suddenly appearing and then vanishing into thin air. I was miked up as I had a few robotic lines to say to the Doctor, so had to be careful what I said off set, as everyone would have been able to hear me.

Sadly for me, the lines were later dubbed by another actor, Geoffrey Beevers. Melkur killed people with his laser eyes and despite the special effects being put on after filming, during breaks I was left well alone by the cast and crew who seemed to find my presence a little intimidating. Getting in and out of the costume was so time consuming that I would have to stay 'in character' for the entire day. With no one daring to speak to me, I would end up having a little kip in the corner until I was needed.

When you were in those costumes you really had to use your imagination as you spent most of the time peeping through a small piece of guaze. Luckily I have a very vivid imagination which went into overdrive when I was chasing the Doctor.

I suppose my greatest claim to fame in the world of *Doctor Who* was playing a Cyberman, when all of the Cybermen were actually played by actors and not just a few with the rest computer generated to make up the numbers like they are these days. I was in a story called Earthshock with Peter Davison, now ensconced in the role of the Doctor. The Cybermen were being particularly evil in this one by planning to blow up a peace conference. Sadly I didn't have any lines but stomping around like a *Star Wars* storm trooper, brandishing a laser gun was a real blast. Although I didn't feel much like a menacing Cyberman when I had to run into Wood Lane, just outside Television Centre, to stop my car from being towed away. And yes I did get some very funny looks.

Filming took place at BBC Television Centre in November 1981 and the guest star for the story was veteran comedienne Beryl Reid. Unfortunately I didn't get to meet her but I did do some scenes with Peter Davison who was a lovely man. Back then he was the youngest Doctor at 29 but of course his record has been broken since by new boy, Matt Smith at 26.

Once again, I received a delightful letter:

*26th January 1982*

*Dear Graham*

*Thanks again for your hard work and patience on the Dr Who story 'Earthshock. I am sure the costumes were extremely uncomfortable to wear however, they have made you all the most spectacular Cybermen that have ever appeared in the series. Without editing the programme, it already promises to be very exciting. Once more, congratulations on your endurance and I hope we can work together again.*

*Yours,*
*Peter Grimwade,*
*Director,*
*Doctor Who*

Eat your heart out Cybermen wannabes. From time to time I attend *Doctor Who* conventions and sign pictures of Marshmen and Cybermen. In all honesty it could be anyone inside those costumes but the fans seem delighted. At least when I watch the *Doctor Who* episodes where I appear as a Cyberman, I can pick myself out as I always made sure I was at the front. Sometimes the fans kindly point out that while there were plenty of Marshmen and Cybermen, there was only ever one Melkur, as they thrust a photo of him under my nose for signing. For some unknown reason they also request signed pictures of Tony Stamp.

I've also attended sci-fi conventions where guests have included, bizarrely, *The Man from U.N.C.L.E* star Robert Vaughan, who nowadays is in the BBC drama *Hustle* and Richard Kiel, who played metal-toothed Jaws in a couple of Roger Moore's James Bond films. I was once situated opposite a couple of actors who had played various alien creatures in *Star Wars*. They had fancy table cloths with their names embroidered on and their table was sprawled with *Star Wars* memorabilia and DVDs. They had a queue of nine. Mine was four.

I don't regret never playing a Dalek. I think I was too bulky to fit into one. There was a small seat inside that I would have struggled to sit comfortably on. And anyway, how boring in comparison to Melkur or a Cyberman. All they did was whizz around yelling "Exterminate Exerminate!" Didn't scare me. The only time I got to see the Daleks in action was when I played a crewmember in the 1984 story The Resurrection of the Daleks, which starred Rula Lenska and also featured Leslie Grantham

I look really long in this picture...

I think I'm a judge.

Canvey Island - when these trunks got wet they got really heavy.

Mum and Dad.

My parents on their wedding day - my Dad married without his suit.

Butter wouldn't melt!

I was thin once - a passport picture but it could be a mug shot...!

With Mum and Dad on my 21st birthday.

The escapologist who couldn't.

A early picture of me in uniform tending to the escapologist.

My gigolo look...

My cabaret look...

If the cap fits...or doesn't in this case!

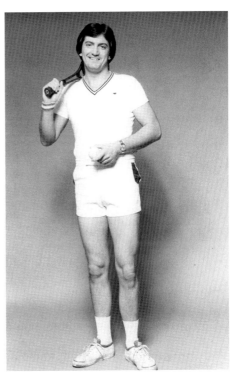

My sporting life....

Becoming a Marshman.                                    Pretty scary, eh?

**BBC tv**

BRITISH BROADCASTING CORPORATION

TELEVISION CENTRE  WOOD LANE  LONDON W12 7RJ

TELEPHONE 01-743 8000   TELEX: 265781

Ex2289

TELEGRAMS AND CABLES: TELECASTS LONDON TELEX

8th September 1980

Grahame Cole Esq.,
c/o  The David Agency,
153 Battersea Rise,
London SW11 1HP

Dear Grahame,

   A brief note to say thank you for putting
up with the discomfort of the latest monster
costume.  I appreciate that it is a tiring and
often thankless task to be part of the fantasy
of the costume department.  But in "Dr. Who" it is
one of the most important elements of the programme,
and I am grateful for all your patience and
stamina during both the filming and the studio
days.

   With all best wishes,

   *Peter*

   (Peter Grimwade)

Hello sailor!

When I first saw Cherry 1974.

Cherry and I outside my Redcoat chalet at
Maddisons, Camber Sands.

The Kevin Keegan look....

As Caiaphas in Jesus Christ Superstar - I must have been about seven feet tall with that hat.

Another legend - Christopher Lee.

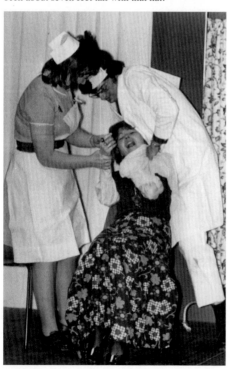

A hospital show or is it just a typical day on the ward...?

Nice legs...!

who went on to play Dirty Den in *EastEnders*.

I was also in a four-part story called Kinda. It was just a small role as a native and I remember that me and my fellow extras had to wear sarongs. The story, which involved a snake which became huge in the final episode, had a great cast including Nerys Hughes, Richard Todd, a real-life hero of D-Day and star of films like *The Dam Busters* and *The Longest Day* and Anna Wing, who went on to play Lou Beale in *EastEnders*.

Jeff Stewart, who played PC Reg Hollis in *The Bill*, was in it playing a character called Dukkha, although his scenes were supposed to be in another world so we never met and Simon Rouse, who plays Chief Inspector Jack Meadows in *The Bill*, was Hindle and I don't remember meeting him either as I don't think we were ever in the same scene.

Apparently I was also in The Twin Dilemma in 1984 with Colin Baker, playing a Jocandan Guard but that seems to have been erased from my memory too! I was also back playing a Cyberman in the 1983 20th anniversary special The Five Doctors and old Melkur made another appearance but they used old footage of me so that doesn't really count.

Looking back I probably should have claimed danger money for some of those *Doctor Who* capers. Certainly it's something I definitely should have done for my next job.

Showbiz legend Eric Sykes was making one of his silent films for Thames Television called *If You Go Down to the Woods Today* and I was hired to play Jefferson, a butch hard-nut soldier who was kitted out in fatigues and constantly chewing gum. Eric was a Scout leader, who along with his troupe, has set up camp in the woods when they stumble across bags of hidden cash. Jefferson assists the police in fighting the gang of bank robbers who are trying desperately to get their loot back.

For this particular scene we were on location in some woods at Wisley in Surrey. I was up a tree, armed with a machine gun and the branches were rigged up for simulated gunfire. As I fired back at the bank robbers, the gun shots were meant to go off one by one. Unfortunately they all exploded at the same time, making an almighty din. I realised I was hurt but it wasn't until I began climbing down the stepladder that my legs started to throb.

Now Eric Sykes is deaf and he thought the scene was perfect, so simply said "Thank you very much, that's a wrap," and moved on. However, when I inspected my legs, they looked pretty nasty as some pieces of tree bark had embedded themselves under the skin. The first assistant director suggested, dismissively, that I see my own doctor but I replied, "I don't think so," so the location manager took me to nearby Kingston Hospital. And am I glad he did.

It took three visits to casualty before they managed to get all the bark out. If they hadn't, the bark might have gone rotten in my legs and caused septicaemia. For several weeks I could barely walk so, of course, I couldn't work. I decided to contact my union Equity after others advised me that if I wanted to work for Thames Television again, (which I would do when I later joined *The Bill*), I shouldn't make a fuss. Just play it softly, softly. So I did and in the end Thames paid me my daily rate for the visits to the hospital plus another fee. To this day I still have the scars. Today, of course, I would probably have sued.

Kenny Everett is rightly revered as a comic genius and I was lucky enough to appear in an edition of *The Kenny Everett Video Show* around this time, the early eighties. In the sketch, I am hiding in the bedroom wardrobe after Kenny, who is playing the lovely Lulu's hubby and looking resplendent in a business suit and bowler hat, comes home unexpectedly. Lulu denies there's another man but Kenny starts frantically searching. Inevitably he finds me and asks, "What are you doing in there?" without batting an eyelid, I calmly answer, "Waiting for a bus," and with that, a double-decker bus comes crashing through the wall and I hop on it. It had to be done in one take so I was terrified of getting my line wrong. For some reason, and most actors agree, having just one line can be harder than a whole speech. The sketch is on YouTube and several people have asked if it's me so yes, it is. Now television crews can be a hard bunch to please but whenever you watch an episode of one of Kenny's shows, you can always hear them laughing in the background. That shows you just how funny and much loved, Kenny was.

One of the strangest gigs I ever did had nothing to do with acting. It was 1983 and Hammer Films, who were famous for their horror movies, were making a film called *House of the Long Shadows* and seeking minders to look after one of the films' three older stars. The job involved driving the star to and from rehearsals and the set; helping them with their lines and taking them wherever they wanted to go on their days off. Basically it was looking after them. It was five weeks work and well paid. The production company would only tell me who these stars were once I had said yes.

I was intrigued and then delighted when, having agreed, I was told that I had a choice between Vincent Price, Peter Cushing or Christopher Lee. All three were Hammer Films' icons and I felt spoilt for choice. It was a close call but I chose Vincent as to me, he reeked of old Hollywood.

*House of the Long Shadows* was a truly terrible film. The leading man was Desi Arnaz Jr, the son of Lucille Ball and Desi Arnaz. He played a writer who bets that he can write a best-selling novel in 24 hours. To get him in the mood, he goes to a remote, deserted Welsh manor. Expecting it to be empty, he is surprised to find Lord Grisbane and his daughter in residence. As the stormy night unfolds, more of the Grisbane family arrive. Naturally, being a horror film, there's something nasty in the attic, waiting to be unleashed.

Despite being a poor film, *House of the Long Shadows* does have a couple of touching claims to fame. It was the only time Christopher Lee, Peter Cushing, Vincent Price and another master of terror, John Carradine appeared in a film together. John Carradine, father of David Carradine, who starred in the seventies TV series *Kung Fu* could quote every single line of dialogue he had ever had. Once, I went to meet his wife at the airport and as John was pretty ancient and riddled with arthritis by then, I was expecting a frail old lady. Imagine my surprise when a busty blonde turned up. The film was also the last time Christopher Lee and Peter Cushing appeared together.

For me, the quality of the film was irrelevant. It was five weeks of bliss. Hanging around the set, watching these guys at work, I often had to pinch myself that this was for real. Here I was, a film fanatic from Essex on a bona fide movie set with a quartet of master craftsman. The manor was actually a stately home in Surrey so Vincent was based in London. He was a real gent. Every day I would pick him up from the Savoy Hotel and he would sit in the front, chatting away. He loved it if I sped down the A3. He'd laugh and say, "Oh, it's just like being Steve McQueen in that movie *Bullitt*." If he wasn't filming, he would pass me little notes with the names of obscure antiques shops or art galleries which he would like to visit. If he bought anything, I would arrange for it to be shipped back to the states for him.

At times the entire experience was truly surreal. Once, Christopher Lee's car didn't turn up so I had Dracula himself and Vincent in the back of the car. When I pulled up at some traffic lights, the startled look on people's faces was a sight to behold. After all, these were two of the scariest men in the world. Both the stars thought it was hilarious.

Peter Cushing was a wonderful man but frail and there was an air of melancholy about him. One weekend, Peter was planning to take the train to his cottage on the Kent coast but I insisted on driving him. When we arrived, he tried to give me some money but I refused, telling him it had been a privilege. As he got out of the car, with his little brown suitcase, and headed for the dark cottage, he looked so sad. I later discovered that his wife had died

10 years earlier and all he wanted to do was go and join her.

Much later, when he learnt I was about to become a father, he wrote me a lovely letter:

*Dear Graham*

*I was deeply touched by your compassionate thoughts. What delightful news about your impending parenthood. Congratulations to you and your wife.*

*May God's blessing be with you always.*

*Kindest regards,*
*Peter Cushing*

As you have probably deduced, after turning Cherry down not once but three times, always replying, "No, not yet," I'd decided to finally make an honest woman of her and this time I asked her. I'd turned her down before because I didn't feel I was really mature enough to get married and also because I didn't think I was yet in a financial position to be able to provide a comfortable home for us and any children we might have. Every time I had turned her down, she would cry buckets and I would feel so guilty for causing her so much pain. Pursuing an acting career meant that I didn't feel that I could offer her the stability I believed she deserved. In my mind we were married anyway but I know that like most women, Cherry was yearning for some kind of stability and commitment. I had never doubted that she was the only woman for me but I also knew that she wanted a traditional wedding, a house and kids and I wasn't sure if I could ever give her those things. Acting is a selfish profession, always putting yourself first. And I had already shown where my loyalties lay when I was unable to be best man at Cherry's brother's wedding, due to work commitments. Generously, Cherry says that she has always known that she comes third after God and the job.

And then it finally dawned on me. If I didn't get my act together, she might do a runner. I realised that life without Cherry wouldn't be worth living. Now it was time to do the honourable thing. And anyway there was no one else for me and one day I wanted her to be the mother of my children. And no way did I want them out of wedlock. So in October 1975 I asked her.

We were in an Italian restaurant, a truly lovely romantic setting, and Cherry didn't have a clue. She just thought we were going out for a nice meal. All of a sudden I got down on one knee, gently took her hand and asked, "Cherry will you marry me?" Stunned, fortunately for me, Cherry didn't hesitate and cried a resounding, "Yes!" And the entire restaurant gave us a standing ovation. The tears, along with the champagne, certainly flowed that night. And Cherry was the happiest I had ever seen her. The next day we bought the ring with as much money as we could gather together and Cherry still has it. Nothing in the world would part her from that precious ring.

But even then we were engaged for a further eight years as I still felt I couldn't look after her properly. I loved Cherry and knew that this was the woman I wanted to spend the rest of my life with. Yet in my heart I still wasn't ready to settle down. Acting is like a drug and can make you incredibly selfish. And living with an actor can be painful. When you take on a role, part of you becomes that character and it can be like living with two different people. As an actor you just can't help it. You immerse yourself in the part, and sometimes take on characteristics which are not particularly nice, while your partner is still living in the real world. Then there was the travelling. I was up and down the country appearing in various theatre productions, leaving Cherry at home. I remember one time getting a phone call from Cherry at the stage door during the interval of a play. She desperately needed to talk to me as she felt she couldn't go on like this but I had to suddenly end the conversation as I was due back on stage. My heart was breaking but I had to carry on and entertain over a thousand people as though I didn't have a care in the world. The moment I came off stage I rushed to a phone box and phoned her back pleading with her and telling her over and over again how much I loved her. Luckily for me, Cherry stuck with me and I can never thank her enough for all the love and support she has given me over the years.

Our courtship had been far from smooth. Not only because of my being here, there and everywhere, but my Mum and Cherry simply didn't get on; just like my grandmother had disapproved of her daughter in-law. In this case it was simply a clash of personalities. And I don't think anyone would have been good enough for her beloved son. It didn't help that Cherry wasn't from the inner circle which included the Church and North West London. A typical example of Mum's bad behaviour was when Cherry would come round for tea. Mum would offer everyone a cuppa except Cherry. "A cup of tea, dad? Graham? Uncle Tom Cobley and all?" while deliberately ignoring Cherry. Both of us were mortified and I would chastise Mum but she would claim I was imagining it.

Another time Mum chased me up the stairs brandishing a broom handle after learning that Cherry was coming to stay with me for an entire summer season. I could feel the broom prodding me as I ran upstairs. I tried to convince her that just because we were sharing a bed didn't mean anything would happen. But she was having none of it.

All that time Cherry never said a word. She has since told me that what kept her going, was knowing that, "He's mine and there's nothing you can do about it..." And in the end my sister Pat, who got on really well with Cherry, told her to forget it. It wasn't worth getting upset about. Dad, on the other hand, welcomed Cherry with open arms. But once again he wouldn't allow any of us to cross Mum.

I didn't have a stag night as it was a novelty for me to spend an evening at home. Besides, my best man was working as were a lot of my mates so there was no one to organise anything which I didn't mind about one bit. Our wedding day was definitely the happiest day of my life. Cherry had bought the dress three years earlier and the pair of us paid for everything as neither of our parents had any money. We had the full church wedding at St

Mary's Church in Hayes, Kent on 9th April 1983. I recall the vicar, Peter Thomas, who knew us both really well, which made an enormous difference, saying that when you hear the Wedding March, turn around and take a look at your bride as she walks down the aisle, as that is a moment you will remember for the rest of your life. So I did, and he was right. I still well up just thinking about it. But despite the sense of tradition, being a modern woman, there was no way Cherry was going to say "Obey."

For a few moments on our wedding day I wondered if it was actually going to happen as Cherry was 35 minutes late, which was a bit too long for my liking. It turned out her mum couldn't get her hat on properly. Another hiccup was push starting the Rolls Royce to the church. But nothing could dampen our day. Just signing the register as Mr and Mrs gave me the biggest thrill. Still does.

On the way to the reception I turned to Cherry and said, "Can't we just keep going?" But we had a great time. We invited about 250 guests and paid for everything ourselves. It was family first and then, at 8pm we were joined by friends. Even my Mum had a lovely time and managed to behave herself all day except shedding a copious amount of tears when I said "I do." A couple of years ago we renewed our vows at the same church with the same vicar. Matthew and Laura were the only witnesses and we recreated the shot of us turning round as we exited the church. We wanted to re-commit to each other. And the magic was and is still there.

By now we had saved enough money for a deposit on a flat

but when I asked Cherry what her dream was, she replied, "A honeymoon in Hawaii." So we decided to blow the lot on just that. We stayed for five weeks, travelling from island to island and it was brilliant. During our time in Hawaii, we visited the famous beach on Kauai Island, where Burt Lancaster and Debra Kerr romped in the fifties film *From Here to Eternity*. There are signs everywhere telling you not to copy the scene but we couldn't resist. Nine months later Matthew was born and swears that he is a Hawaiian baby. We had a fantastic time and when we came back, we set up home in a rented house in South Norwood. Cherry had been on the council list for years but never got higher than 85.

I am so glad we threw caution to the wind. I lost my sister Pat in 2005 to cancer. I used to ask her to come with us when we visited Australia and she would always reply, "Maybe next year." And then suddenly there wasn't a next year. Pat was one of those people who never reached her full potential. She was really bright and passed the eleven plus. She married quite young, as people used to do and moved to Cambridgeshire. While bringing up two daughters, she managed to hold down a job as a top PA in a major multi-national company.

For four years she had been treated for what the doctors thought was Crohn's, an inflammatory disease of the intestines, when they suddenly realised it was actually bowel cancer. Pat immediately began chemotherapy but by then the disease had a firm grip. My sister Jill was always there for Pat as was Cherry and they regularly talked on the phone. Once Pat rang Cherry up saying she was lying on the sofa and feeling awful. What was making it worse was Doug, her husband, was due in soon and would be expecting his dinner on the table and would start moaning if it wasn't. Both Cherry and I were furious. He died recently too but I could never forget what my sister had told me. We decided to have Pat stay for a couple of weeks so that she could get some proper rest. But already I could see that the light was going out of her eyes and she was starting to give up the fight. It wasn't helped by her nurse's childcare issues. Sometimes when Pat was in pain and would ring for help, the nurse wasn't always able to visit, which was exasperating.

For a while the disease seemed to be under control thanks to a load of pills. But then Pat started to go downhill and was finally admitted to a hospice. When we arrived to see her I was struck by how tired and drawn she looked and she had become very thin. She smiled and said, "Don't worry, I'm only here so that they can sort out my medication..." But we knew it was only a matter of time. I've always been an advocate of hospices but I wasn't very impressed when they moved Pat into a ward full of old people who were close to dying.

We were told that she wouldn't survive more than two days but it proved to be slightly longer. Fortunately the hospice had a room we could stay in. Jill's husband Derek and I were dispatched to get some new knickers. Being spotted in a lingerie department meant a small crowd soon formed as we haplessly tried to choose the right underwear. In the end we returned with one or two pairs of enormous bloomers just for a joke to lighten the atmosphere at

Pat's bedside, as well as the items she needed.

As Pat drifted in and out of consciousness, all we could do was dip a stick sponge in water and help her to suck on it. And talk to her, reminiscing, anxiously attempting to keep things as light as possible. She was on a morphine drip but I could see the pain on her face. When I asked the doctor how much longer does she have to suffer, he matter of factly replied, "The only thing wrong with her is the cancer and we have to wait for that to poison her other organs..." Thanks.

After four days of waiting helplessly by my sister's side, it all became too much and I recall that I just sat in an armchair and cried and cried for an hour and a half. And even then there was no privacy. As I looked up I could see people staring at me. I can honestly say it was one of the worst experiences of my life. Watching someone you love suffering a lingering death is too awful for words. You wouldn't do that to an animal would you? Pat later died in her husband's arms while I had to return to *The Bill* and get back to work.

I was away on tour as usual when Cherry discovered she was pregnant. So she bought two little booties with the intention of presenting them to me when she came to visit. But she was so ill that in the end she had to tell me over the phone which was a real shame.

Cherry was sickly throughout both her pregnancies. While carrying Matthew she had hyperemesis gravidarum, an extreme form of morning sickness. Morning, noon and night, she couldn't stop vomiting. During the pregnancy she was hospitalised about 10 times. We tried every remedy we could think of, food, whatever craving she wanted, to try to keep her fluids up. Just before Matthew was born on February 5th 1984, Cherry, who is 5 feet 7 tall, weighed barely seven stone. Yet the moment she gave birth, she didn't feel sick anymore, only elation at being a mum. She was so happy she even got up and made everyone on the ward cups of tea, her horrendous sickness already a distant memory.

I was determined to be at my child's birth so was with her the entire time she was in labour. But it was incredibly hard to see Cherry in such agony, knowing there was nothing I could do. As usual I tried to keep everyone's spirits up but Cherry told me off for talking to the nurses too much. I cannot describe the sense of wonder as I watched Matthew come into this world. His little head and tiny body were just perfect. Becoming a dad for the first time was life changing and after his birth, being a soppy old thing, I re-enacted that scene from the seventies TV mini-series, *Roots* when Kunta Kinte holds his baby up to the sky and thanks God.

Cherry and I had always wanted at least four children and were reassured that she wouldn't get ill a second time. They knew what it was and it wouldn't happen again. But it did. We had decided not to leave it too long after Matthew's birth and less than a year later, Cherry was pregnant again. And within days the vomiting was back and despite their promises, the doctors couldn't stop it. Her hormones were all over the place and I don't think they have ever been the same since.

Not content with throwing up all over the place, Cherry managed to fall down the stairs from the very top all the way down to the bottom, half way through the nine months. The hall walls were covered in blood and we were convinced she had lost the baby. Rushed to hospital, it turned out that the only injury was a severely bashed toe. The baby was fine despite the medical staff insisting it was too small. There was even speculation that it might be born seriously ill or with a disability. Luckily Cherry and I had our faith and we just knew that this wasn't the case.

But her weight had plummeted from eight and a half stone to just over seven and it was clear Cherry was struggling so it was decided to keep her in hospital for a while. Matthew was still a tiny tot and back then other children weren't allowed to stay in hospital. So when I'd take him to visit his mother, he didn't know who she was which was very upsetting for Cherry. During that time my Mum proved a tower of strength. In spite of her antipathy towards Cherry she came to stay and looked after Matthew.

Going into labour the second time round proved to be a trial. We were at a friend's party when Cherry's waters broke. She was mortified but even worse there were no contractions so for a few days she had to lie in a hospital bed waiting for nature to take its course. By this time I was in *The Bill* and as Cherry was pushing with all her might to bring our second child a into the world, all the doctors and nurses seemed interested in was, "What's it like being in *The Bill*?" and despite, still being little more than a 'walk on,' "Could I have your autograph?"

Laura arrived on October 28th 1985 and proved a healthy

10lb whopper. We named her after Laura Collins whose party we had been attending when Cherry's waters broke. Born late at night, Cherry didn't have any visitors for two days other than Mum, Matthew and me. Apparently that's normal with the second baby; the novelty has worn off. I'm pleased to say that has never been the case with either Cherry or myself. Being a parent is a blessing.

I have always felt bad about what Cherry went through during both her pregnancies. I was away most of the time touring when she was carrying Matthew. And she was so ill both times. We had planned to have more children but after giving birth to Laura, Cherry was warned that she could die if she tried to have anymore and advised to have a hysterectomy. I thank God that we had a healthy girl and boy and that I still have Cherry.

With our expanding family, it seemed a good time to think about moving somewhere bigger. The first place we'd bought was through a housing association which meant we owned half. It was a lovely cottage in Bromley, Kent, built for railway workers at the turn of the 20th century. While we just had Matthew, it was just about feasible for Cherry and the baby to come and stay with me in the caravan at weekends. But with two very young children it was now impossible. Money was always tight and even when Cherry was pregnant, she had pounded the streets delivering local newspapers.

With me being away so much, she would drop the kids off at nursery in the morning so that she could work at home doing upholstery and making curtains, a skill she'd learned by doing a three-year apprenticeship. She's a real whizz at that stuff. Then she would collect them, give them their tea and their bath and put them to bed, all on her own. I cannot tell you how guilty I feel to this day. There was I living the dream and there was Cherry bringing up our family alone without any support network other than the odd visit from both our mums.

Acting work remained steady and I even had a tiny part in the third Indiana Jones film, *The Last Crusade*. I played a Russian who arrests Indy, knocking his famous hat off in the process. Being on the set of such a huge movie was another great experience. Harrison Ford was very down to earth. We filmed the scene at a stately home that was playing the school where Indy was supposed to be teaching at and I remember walking onto the set with him. He said he'd never stopped getting excited about going on set and seeing what all the carpenters and the rest of the crew had created in advance of filming starting. He was a carpenter before becoming an actor and I think he was still fascinated by the set construction and the preparation that goes on before filming. Of course, he was a huge star but he seemed very unaffected by fame and was very chatty and made the people around him feel at ease.

Back in 1979 I'd had a tiny role in the BBC spy drama *Tinker, Tailor, Soldier, Spy* with Sir Alec Guinness, another huge star and he was also very down to earth. He was absolutely lovely. We filmed at a warehouse somewhere and during a tea break, I found myself standing up a few feet away from him. There was a chair next to him and he said: "Sit down, sit down." I was completely in awe of him.

I was also continuing to hone my stage fighting skills. When I was appearing in a production of *Cabaret*, I was Nazi agitator, Ernest Ludwig, who had to have a fight with Clifford Bradshaw, the American who is visiting Berlin. The part was played by Michael York in the film but here it was by an actor called Julian Cope. Julian wasn't a great stage fighter and during rehearsals he would always catch me somewhere.

On opening night, he managed to catch me on the nose. My eyes started watering and my nose started bleeding. So at the end of Act One, when I stood up to sing the haunting song, Tomorrow Belongs to Me, I couldn't see a thing as there were both blood and tears streaming down my face. The next day the review read, 'Graham Cole manages to ring a huge amount of emotion out of the piece'. If only he had known how much it had really cost me.

# CHAPTER SIX

# Reporting for Duty

Thames Television's *The Bill* had made its debut in the autumn of 1983 as a one-off pilot called *Woodentop*. Featuring a baby-faced Mark Wingett as PC Jim Carver and Trudie Goodwin as PC June Ackland, the story focused on Carver's first day on the job. Peter Dean, who later found fame in *EastEnders* playing Pete Beale, was Sergeant Wilding. Written by Geoff McQueen, the show had been an instant hit and a full series was commissioned.

So in 1984 Thames began filming eight one-hour episodes. And, thanks to casting director Julian Oldfield, I was brought in as an extra, due mainly to my stage fighting skills. From day one I was cast as a copper and it was a strange feeling the first time I put on the uniform. It was quite heavy, what with all the extra gear attached including the radio, a pair of handcuffs and a truncheon. At first the handcuffs used to be real but following a series of jolly japes, involving cast and crew being cuffed either together or onto railings, and accidentally on purpose losing the key, they are now firmly welded shut. The outfit really did give you a sense of power and pride.

My first appearance was in an episode called Drugs Raid. I played an officer sent in to break up a fight. I was actually a 'walk on,' which is one step up from being an extra. Rather than milling around in the background, it's basically an acting role without any words. Following this first outing as a policeman, Jennie Tate, the head of wardrobe, kept calling me back in; apparently she thought I was sweet and that I looked like a real copper. I have a lot to thank Jennie for.

Once again, it was just a job to me but I enjoyed it and as there was only one series a year, I could still combine *The Bill* with theatre work and the odd other TV role including an anaesthetist in medical drama, *Casualty*. In those days the set was housed in an old warehouse, located in Artichoke Hill in Wapping, East London. Right next door to News International, the home of The Sun newspaper. During the infamous union disputes in the eighties, the area was often reminiscent of a riot scene out of *The Bill*.

I have never been very good at being in the background so whatever scene I was in, I would intentionally break the cardinal rule of being an extra which is 'Don't draw attention to yourself.' It wasn't necessarily to be noticed, more a case of having something to do and injecting my role, however minor, with a bit of creativity. So whenever another character passed me by I was always doing something deliberately wrong, from putting my feet up on the desk to chewing gum and spitting it in the bin. Years later I read that when Linda Gray was cast as Sue Ellen in *Dallas* it was only a small part. But whenever she was in a scene with JR, she gave him such a look of pure hatred, that the producers noticed and her part was made bigger. I don't know if what I was up to got me noticed but I don't think it did me any harm.

I also started doing some driving in *The Bill*. I'd mentioned that I had a racing licence from my days of doing a spot of stock car racing, as well as my stint as an ambulance driver. So from time to time I would drive one of the area cars in chase sequences. Being a petrol head, I thought I had died and gone to heaven.

Early on in my time at *The Bill*, I was in the middle of filming a long chase sequence. In fact it was one of my first speaking scenes when one of the crew handed me a note. It simply said, "Cherry in hospital." It was during the time Cherry was pregnant with our daughter Laura so I was worried sick and couldn't understand what had happened. Obviously the note was brief and didn't mention any reason or even which hospital. Unfortunately I couldn't leave the set until the scene was finished. But after rushing up and down Shepherds Bush market, two or three times, chasing some toe rag, I said enough is enough and rushed off to see her. When I finally got to the hospital, I was told Cherry had fallen down the stairs. Thankfully Cherry and the baby were fine.

After a couple of years as a seen but never heard presence in *The Bill*, my character at last had a name, PC Tony Stamp, thanks to the writers and was first mentioned in the episode Some you Win, Some you Lose in 1987. However, it was my driving skills that led to my breakthrough. After three years as a highly successful TV show, there were plans afoot to make a few changes to *The Bill*. It would cease being a series consisting of eight one-hour episodes, once a year, and become a half-hour format, broadcast twice a week, all year round. The producers felt that the show needed to be more exciting and realised that increasing the number of car chases was one solution. A cameraman asked me if I would be interested in helping out with some camera tests. Naturally I said yes. The assignment involved driving a Rover around the streets of London for three weeks, with a camera strapped to the side of the car, and a cameraman in the back along with all his gear. My job was to drive the car around, sometimes at top speed and do twists and turns to see firstly if the camera stayed attached, and secondly whether the shots were good enough to use. Third was whether the cameraman could refrain from throwing up.

Unbeknown to me, Rolie Luker the cameraman I was working with, was reporting back to base that, "This guy is great, really uncomplicated and happy to do anything." Anyway, this got back to Peter Cregeen, the executive producer who called me into his office. Peter was a lovely man and said, "Graham, I have been hearing very good things about you and how much you helped with the camera tests. And as a thank you, I would like to give you a few lines in a forthcoming episode and see how it goes from there."

He had always been enormously supportive in the past, writing kind letters of thanks and assuring me, "If there is anything, it will probably be tiny at first, but at least it would be a foot in door." Now, here he was, as good as his word.

I was gobsmacked but determined to ensure whatever lines I was given made an impact. I knew it was make or break time. Blow your lines and you could say ta ta to any more; get them right and who knows? The episode was called Light Duties and featured the debut of a new Inspector, Christine Fraser, played by Barbara Thorn. My character is dealing with a disturbance on the streets, along with PC Taffy Edwards (Colin Blumentheau) when a lady comes up to me offering her assistance. Dismissively, I deliver my first ever line on *The Bill*, "Thank you very much madam but would you mind going on your way." Later at parade, Stamp is mortified when that same lady is introduced as the new Inspector.

In another scene with Barbara, to emphasise the trouble Inspector Fraser is having in a man's world, I am sitting at a desk and on the phone, when she asks to me stand up. I do so, very slowly to emphasise just how much I end up towering over her. I was deliberately asked to do that scene so that viewers could get an idea, metaphorically speaking, of exactly what this female Inspector was up against in this man's world.

I hoped I had done well enough maybe to get a few more lines but I was a realist. As far as I could see *The Bill* had its main cast, I doubted there was room for another uniformed character and CID was bulging at the seams. So I was surprised when I got a call from Peter inviting me to the launch of the half hours. And I was even more surprised when I turned up to find a picture of myself in the press pack and a blurb about one PC Tony Stamp. I still didn't have an agent and nobody had formally approached me about becoming a regular. Plus I had just signed up for a 12-week stint in the musical *Guys and Dolls* in Leicester playing the Lieutenant. But I knew that more than anything, I wanted to be part of *The Bill*. Fortunately casting director Julian Oldfield came to my rescue and after a few phone calls he got me out of the musical.

So here I was, on a Monday morning, doing the read through of my first episode as bona fide PC Tony Stamp. Although I knew all my colleagues, I couldn't quite believe that I was now the equal of Eric Richard (Sergeant Bob Cryer), Trudie Goodwin (PC June Ackland), John Salthouse (Detective Inspector Roy Galloway) and Tony Scannell (Detective Sergeant Ted Roach). They were all enormously supportive of me and made me feel very welcome.

Little did I know that this was a role I would play for well over 20 years. Actors talk about needing to play different parts, but for me, no two days or even scenes were ever the same on *The Bill*.

The show had been forced to move from Wapping, party due to the lengthy strikes at the news plant next door but also because more space was needed to accommodate the extra cast and crew who had joined for the extra number of episodes. The situation had got so bad that often uniformed actors had been mistaken for real police officers and attacked. Hence in the late eighties *The Bill* set up shop in a former record company distribution depot in Barlby Road, North Kensington. When the lease on the Victorian building ran out in 1989 the owners decided to turn the site into a shopping centre, so in 1990 *The Bill* moved again. This time it was from Barlby Road to Deer Park Road in Merton, South London and that is where the studios remain to this day.

The producers got around the new look by having a storyline in which much of Sun Hill was blown up by a terrorist bomb, which meant that afterwards the station had to undergo some major building work. Popular PC Ken Melvin was killed in the blast and Tony Stamp was asked to deliver the eulogy at his funeral. Mark Powley, the actor who played him, was a lovely bloke and had decided that he was ready to leave so was happy to be the sacrificial lamb. He's a great actor and a good guy to be around. I spotted him recently in a BBC sitcom called *Life of Riley* playing, would you believe, Caroline Quentin's ex-husband. But he will always be remembered as the first regular *Bill* character to be killed off.

Ben Roberts, who played Inspector Derek Conway, was a terrible giggler and it took us hours to film the scene where he asks Stamp if he will do the reading at the funeral. Every time I looked at Ben, he had this glint in his eye, and the pair of us would burst out laughing. Later, when we filmed the eulogy scene, it was even harder to keep a straight face as Mark Powley had slipped in unnoticed and was standing at the back grinning at me. When I spotted him it really did feel like I was seeing a ghost.

The outside of Bosun House, our new base, named after executive producer Michael Chapman's dog, looked rather grim and you would never believe that it was home to a top television show. But inside it's a powerhouse of activity. The layout is like a rabbit warren and it was easy to get lost. Initially, as you walk through, there are offices and a large canteen, where the food was - unbelievably - free. This harks back to the days when the set-up was regarded as a location. If you are filming away from the studio, the food is always free.

It all looks straightforward enough until you turn a few corners and start entering another world altogether. Suddenly you are in the wards of St Hugh's Hospital, all spick and span; next door is a courtroom where Stamp stood in the dock, accused of knocking down and killing a pedestrian. Further down the corridor is Sun Hill nick itself. Downstairs houses the custody desk and cells, which has been a temporary home to a long list of scumbags. While upstairs houses CID and the Sun Hill top brass. As the set was custom made, some of the areas had been 'dirtied down' to look old and worn in the pursuit of authenticity.

The props department, run by prop master extraordinaire Mr Dave Hodges, is a vast emporium stuffed with naff paintings and endless sets of flying ducks, and nick knacks brought in to dress outside properties hired for filming. And due to the endless stream of extras needed for the show, the wardrobe department has a similar area full of boxes containing shoes of all sizes, hats, scarves and gloves galore plus outfits including nurses' uniforms and flashy gear that ladies of the night might wear.

I spent very little time at base because Stamp was always out on the streets, mostly driving Sierra One, the area car. And that's the way I liked it. The only downside was the weather. Rain or shine, *The Bill* filmed in all weathers. Otherwise, if an episode cannot be transmitted, due to excessive amounts of wind, rain, hail or snow the production can only claim on the insurance if it has at least tried to film the episode. Small crowds always gathered where we were filming and I loved chatting to the public and getting their reaction. And their stories could be just as fascinating and poignant as anything depicted in *The Bill*.

One young couple have stayed in my thoughts since I met them on location in Central London. They were thoroughly enjoying watching us filming and as I signed a photo, I was struck by their bravery. "Our son is in Great Ormond Street Hospital, about to have a major operation and we just needed to get a breath of fresh air," they told me. "To be able to share in something as exciting as this was a real tonic." Listening to that, I was so glad *The Bill* could offer a morsel, no matter how small, of comfort.

For me, the most boring scenes to do were the parade ones, when all we had to do was sit and listen to the Sergeant giving a pep talk before we went on duty. I am not very good at doing nothing. And from time to time my great mate John Bowler (PC Roger Valentine) and I were brought in simply to be in the background of a scene. When I queried this, the producers said, "But the audience like to see you." Surely they'd like to have heard us too?

An average day in the life of Graham Cole changed little over the quarter of a century I was in *The Bill*. Could it really have been that long? If I had an early call I was up at 5.30am and tried not to wake the rest of the house up by singing in the shower. I didn't always have breakfast and tended to take a flask of tea to have in the car as I drove to work. If it was an early call I would listen to Steve Allen on LBC who really made me laugh or Nick Ferrari who more often than not had me shouting back at the radio. Sometimes I listened to Radio 4. I now live just outside Bromley so it took about 40 minutes, that early in the morning, to get to *The Bill* base. I always got in earlier than my call time. I think it was a habit I picked up from the theatre where there was always the real fear that someone might be off sick and alternative plans had to be made, quick. I think it also shows respect for your fellow actors and the crew.

I had my own dressing room but even when I became a regular, I still had to share for a long time. Originally there was one for the girls and one for the boys. We only got individual ones when they partitioned the space. And even then you still had to share with another cast member until you had earned the right to a room all to yourself. It was still quite small but I preferred to think of it as cosy. I like socialising and always enjoyed having a gossip with the girls in the office. Very little went on in that building that I didn't know about but I was the soul of discretion; I really am the sort of person whom you can trust with a secret. Sometimes I would nip in the canteen for a few slices of toast but if I had had a tough week, I'd treat myself to a traditional full English breakfast. I know…but sometimes you just need a bit of stodge.

Like all the police costumes at *The Bill*, mine was kept under lock and key in case, ironically, they got nicked and are used by people to impersonate real police officers. The wardrobe department hire them from the police's own suppliers so they were the real thing. Mine was always laid out in my dressing room, ready for me to put on. The white shirts look a bit dull to the naked eye as they are deliberately washed with a black sock. This is because on screen their whiteness is just too dazzling for the cameras.

Andrew Lancel, who plays DI Neil Manson in CID, always said it was easier for those playing an officer in uniform to find their character than those in civvies. And I think he has a point. The moment I put that uniform on, I was more than halfway towards becoming PC Tony Stamp. I then trotted off to make-up to have a bit of slap put on my face. The make-up department used to dye my hair and I had a real battle on my hands when I suggested they stop as it was beginning to look slightly ridiculous. Like in all serial dramas, you were not allowed to change your hairstyle without permission. So I went to see Pat Sandys, one of the producers, whom I admired enormously and who sadly died in 2000, but she wouldn't hear of it.

"Darling, if you came into a casting, all I would see is the grey hair, it's too ageing." I took it on the chin and the make-up girls tried their best by using vegetable dye to see if that offered a more natural look, but it was even worse. And it washed out really quickly, leading to ridiculous accusations that I was taking, "Too many showers." One day I looked in the mirror and thought enough is enough. So I dragged the head of make-up outside, into the daylight, where Stamp spends most of his time and said, "Look, can you now see how it changes colour outside and looks a right old mess of different shades?" At last she and the producers saw the light.

Interestingly enough I remember one of the make-up girls was very excited after getting a job on *Inspector Morse*. But she was back within three weeks as she couldn't deal with being given a list of what she could and couldn't say to John Thaw. Thankfully *The Bill* was never like that. They really were a fantastic bunch of actors along with a truly amazing crew, who like myself, had worked there for years. And yes, there were some you liked, for example, Trudie Goodwin and Alex Walkinshaw, more than others. But there wasn't really any time for anyone to be a prima donna. The schedule is relentless and using only one camera means there's no time for tantrums or endless re-takes. If you couldn't take the heat, then you needed to get out of the kitchen, fast.

If I was in Bosun House waiting to be called, I spent most of my time in my dressing room catching up on fan mail or making phone calls. Like all productions there was a green room where the actors hung out. But I rarely went in there. I simply couldn't listen to actors moaning about what a hard day they were having. One of them, who I'm afraid must remain nameless for fear of him being lynched, once claimed it was harder playing a policeman than being one. What a complete load of cobblers. Unlike me, some of them didn't seem to realise how lucky they were to be doing a job like this. Acting can be stressful at times, but compared to working as a real police officer or in an accident and emergency department in a hospital it's a walk in the park. I really don't have a lot of time for actors who whinge about how tough the job is.

The runner (whose job, as the title suggests, is to run round making sure people are in the right place at the right time) would come to tell me it was time to get on the bus which would take me out to location. A runner can make or break your life. A good one will stay calm and only come and get you when the crew is actually ready for you. A bad one will panic, knock on the door 10 minutes too early and end up getting himself and you into a totally unnecessary state and force you to hang around on set, endlessly waiting.

I was nearly always the first on the bus and never really understood why some actors revelled in keeping everybody waiting. Maybe it was a power trip. Though thinking about it, it was probably more to do with the cry wolf syndrome. They had been called to the bus so many times by a frantic runner, only to be left sitting there for ages before finally setting off, that they decided to deliberately wait until the very last minute. Whatever the reason, they were always the ones who would moan, near the end of the day, when filming was running late.

The night before filming, I'd learn my lines and study the script. I tended to do that in the privacy of my study. I never liked walking around the house spouting lines. I would make notes in the margin with regard to how I thought I might say the line or questions I would like to ask the director on set. Sometimes a courier would arrive with an amended script or shooting schedule which keeps you on your toes. I liked to know my lines inside out and worked very hard on them as I knew during the day I'd muck about from time to time. I liked to lighten the mood on set as filming can be quite intense. And if I got a line wrong, I couldn't help saying, "Who wrote this rubbish?" It certainly worked every time.

Over the years I've spent a lot of time going out on patrol with the real police for research purposes which has proved to be fascinating. One time when I was out with the cops, we were in an area car going at high speed. We had the blue lights flashing, the siren blaring and then we skidded to a halt. The two real coppers and I leapt out, jumped over a roadside barrier and immediately found ourselves in the thick of a violent brawl between 20 teenage thugs.

But instead of stopping their fighting and running off, the youths turned on us. They were lads from two teenage gangs fighting for territory outside a pizza restaurant in Wimbledon, South West London. The oldest was no more than about 18 and most were only about 15. They were fighting and punching each other and just would not stop. Usually when police arrive and yell at them, they stop fighting and blame each other but these lads just kept going at it.

I got two of them up against a wall, one in each hand, and then one jumped on my back and it was the same for each of the two policemen I was with. It was horrendous - the worst trouble I've ever seen. The lads were trying to radio through for more assistance. It was one hell of a scrap. It was like a cartoon, you'd pull one off the bundle and throw him aside and he'd soon be back in again. It was unbelievable. Eventually we got called off and a van arrived with reinforcements but by that time we'd had a good 20 minutes of physically not being able to stop the fighting. By the end of it one of the two policeman had been smacked in the mouth and had had all his shirt ripped. The other two of us got away with not much more than bruises on the arms and legs and the odd punch in the ear. Being a former rugby player you learn to protect your face, although I've had my nose broken three or four times during games which is why it's such a strange shape. By the end of it, six were arrested.

I used to love going out with the real police. When I first started on the show it used to be me asking them if I could come out to do some research with excruciating crawling phone calls. But after I'd become established they started to ask me which was great and each area used to say they were the busiest division around. But the Metropolitan Police were very careful and they made sure I knew that it was my responsibility if I went out with their officers. They were not officially asking me to do it and the programme didn't ask me to but I felt that it was important to get it right.

If I was out with the real cops and they were in trouble I couldn't just stand back and watch. I remember at one police station this great sergeant said to me: "You've done this before, haven't you?" He went through the usual procedures and then just as he was about leave he turned to me and said: "Oh, and if there's a punch-up, you'll have to make your own arrangements!" I think some of my colleagues thought I was a nutcase because

I used to go out and do the research that I did but I enjoyed it and I really found that it helped. I think it let me pick up lots of the realism that coppers face rather than just doing what the scriptwriters gave me in lines.

Obviously I never wore a uniform when I was out doing research and probably because of that I didn't get recognised very often, although one time someone came up and asked me for my autograph during a mock raid on a house which was rather embarrassing.

My research helped to give me an attitude and a way of approaching things and I think it helped to make Tony Stamp a typical area car driver. Stamp was supposed to be this really experienced, up-front copper, gun trained and martial arts trained. Going out with the police was always terribly exciting – there was no other word for it - and the adrenalin really flowed. I'd sit in the car and chat to the lads and we didn't know what was going to happen; a call could be anything from a fight to an armed robbery.

I remember one time being out with them in Cricklewood and we were called to a bomb alert at this huge pub. It was back in the days when the IRA carried out bombings in London and a call had been made to the landlord about a package. We were the first to arrive, so cleared the pub and then naturally I went in with the lads and started to search for the bomb. I was looking under these chairs on the second floor and I suddenly thought: 'Graham, what are you doing? Supposing you find it?' But you get so caught up in what's going on that you don't really think about things like that and it's the same for police officers. Looking for bombs is not why they joined the police force. On that occasion it was a hoax but it could have been for real.

There was an element of tremendous danger because I didn't know if we were going to find a bomb. Even if one had been discovered, there could have been another and another. We did a story in *The Bill* about an unexploded wartime bomb which had been washed up and that brought the memory of that day flooding back. I hope the fact that I've been out there for real, made my performances better.

In the early hours of one morning, I was out with a couple of lads from Mitcham police station when the guys I was with spotted an Escort XR3i and did a quick U-turn. We got up behind it, radioed through to the nick and they confirmed that it was a stolen vehicle, so we followed it. They stopped and got out and the police driver got hold of the driver but the passenger was off on his toes so the other officer and myself gave chase. We followed him over a couple of fences, then the guy shinned up a wall and onto a garage roof and we followed him up there. We were halfway across a roof when a window opened and someone shouted: "Get off my roof!" The culprit jumped down into a garden and we followed but he disappeared. We searched in vain for him for 30 minutes before calling in a dog handler team. The dogs quickly tracked him down and the two guys were nicked for taking and driving away a car.

On two occasions while I was out with the police, the guys I was with were called on to tackle armed robbers. In those situations I always stayed behind the car because I didn't want to get in the way. I never wanted to make their job any harder than it already was. Another time they were called to deal with a man waving a five-foot samurai sword around. He was going mad and the officers I was with tried to talk to him and calm him down but in the end we withdrew and called in the Territorial Support Group (TSG) who came in with riot shields and arrested him.

Over the years the techniques and hints I learnt from my nights out with the police helped me make Tony Stamp believable. Cherry never liked me going out with the police as she worried that I might not come back but it was never a real cause for concern. Like some of my actor mates, she thought it was a bit strange that I used to do it because it didn't have to be done. But we never argued about it. She never liked me going out at night but, of course, that was always the best time for me to go to talk to the officers. When I was out with them she'd go to bed and still be only half asleep when I'd roll in at about 7.30am.

I've seen the police being forced to take more and more stick from people over the years and it is something that is totally unacceptable. They get a lot of verbal abuse and frankly I don't know how they cope with it. There's a lack of respect these days – not just for the police – but for other people generally and that is something that worries me a great deal. People don't have the time of day for other people which is a sad reflection on society. People are all too willing to walk by on the other side and not get involved and I don't think that is a good thing at all.

Sometimes when I would go onto estates with them they

would get a huge amount of abuse and taunts and it has definitely got worse over the years – as has the violence they face while protecting the rest of us. It can be sickening to witness the way they are sometimes treated. Officers might be bringing someone out of a shop or whatever and there will always be someone there saying: "Why aren't you chasing burglars instead?" without having any idea what the person is being arrested for.

The increase in the carrying of guns, knives, steel bars and other weapons is frightening. Drugs are a huge problem. Kids as young as nine are into them and something like 60 per cent of burglaries, muggings and purse snatches are done just to pay for drug habits.

Episodes of *The Bill* are filmed about three months in advance and up until recently there could be as many as five units, each shooting a separate episode. They were named after a colour so for example, there's the green unit or the red unit and their scripts are coloured accordingly. When executive producer Paul Marquess joined the show in 2002 he banned the coloured scripts, misguidedly thinking it led to some kind of rivalry between the units. For the cast and crew it just became confusing, especially as episodes are not shot in the order of the script. Sometimes I would be shuffling between five units in one day so the coloured scripts helped you keep, just about, on top of things.

But sometimes mistakes got made. Once it was a week since I had been with one particular unit and we were only now shooting the next scene. The director and production assistant asked me to wear an earpiece as I had the radio but I pointed out that last week my partner had the radio, and was therefore wearing the earpiece and I was holding a pair of binoculars. They made a quick phone call back to base and discovered that I was right. It had been eight days since we shot the preceding scene and despite filming other episodes, I still remembered.

You often met the guest artistes for the first time on the bus. *The Bill* is like a modern day rep company and renowned for the quality of the acting talent it attracts. Particular favourites of mine were Ron Moody, who was the original Fagin in *Oliver* and the late Mollie Sugden of *Are you being Served?* fame, who played a couple of elderly con artistes. They were great fun, oozing a sense of mischief both on and off set.

Ron was sharing a dressing room with some other guest artistes so I told him that as I wouldn't be in for a couple of days, he was welcome to use mine. Now I had quite a large bean bag on the floor which I used to lie on and watch TV during breaks. When I returned to my dressing room, a few days later, there was a card from Ron thanking me for the use of the room - but cursing the bean bag. He had been lying on it, perfectly comfortable until he tried to get up and couldn't. He had to shout for help until a couple of burly crew rescued him. Every time I think about Fagin getting stuck on my bean bag, it makes me smile. And in a note left for me, he wrote: "Thank you for the use of your room. But I will avoid the anti-gravity bag in future. Ron."

I have enormous admiration for guest stars as it can't be easy coming in to a show like *The Bill* which is full-on from the word go. From time to time, I deliberately blew my lines to make a guest feel more at ease.

Sometimes the ones you don't expect to be nervous are the worst. Dorothy Tutin was a well respected and experienced stage actress who was playing a doctor's wife, beaten up by her husband. I was walking down a corridor at base, with Seeta Indrani who played PC Norika Datta, (she is now a regular in daytime drama *Doctors*) when Dorothy called me into her dressing room. She promptly burst into tears saying, "I have done two days and I really can't do this. I can't keep up with the pace. They tell me what they want and how they want it and then they tell me they want it now but I just can't do it." I put my arm around her and asked, "What was your first job like?" And she replied, "Terrible." And I said, "But you still came back for more didn't you?" She nodded. "Nothing's changed, you might be a little older but the job's still the same and you can do it." And with that she thanked me, wiped her tears away, regained her composure and accompanied me back onto set where she gave a top notch performance.

On the other hand Jean Boht, who played Nellie Boswell in the sitcom *Bread*, had the time of her life on *The Bill*. She was playing a granny with dementia who had gone walkabout. We were filming in Croydon and the flyover had been shut especially for *The Bill*. Jean had to walk over the flyover, in the middle of the road, with not a care in the world, among all this traffic, now provided by *The Bill*. Sierra One, with me at the helm, had to tear up the road and screech to a halt. Then Stamp had to jump out and pull her onto the pavement before she got knocked over. After the first take, Jean was beside herself. "It is so exciting being rescued by PC Stamp!" she joked.

Hundreds of stars passed through Sun Hill before they were famous. Spice Girl Emma Bunton was a troubled teenager while Paul O'Grady played DS Ted Roache's (Tony Scannell) transvestite snout Roxanne. Anita Dobson, who was Angie Watts in *EastEnders,* played DS Phil Hunter's mum, funnyman Rik Mayall played bad guy Patrick Massie, *House* star Hugh Laurie was a barrister, Robert Carlyle played a journalist and The Who legend Roger Daltrey played a drug dealer, after his friend Billy Murray (DS Don Beech) suggested he appear.

In fact the list of famous faces who have been in *The Bill* reads like a who's who of top British stars: David Walliams, Sean Bean, Martin Kemp, Alex Kingston, Lynda Bellingham, Michelle Collins, Denise Van Outen, Ray Winstone, Eric Sykes, Leslie Ash, Kathy Burke, Leslie Philips and June Brown.

French Footballer Emmanuel Petit also popped up as himself in a 1998 Christmas episode and *GMTV*'s Lorraine Kelly appeared when she interviewed PC Cathy Bradford (Connie Hyde) for a scene.

And who'd have thought that Sheena Rose, the 10-year-old tearaway trying to get away from me in an episode called Swan Song in 1995, would grow up to be Keira Knightley, international film star.

My great pal Alex Walkinshaw also appeared in *The Bill* as a teenage tea leaf who nicked an ice cream van. He got caught by Stamp but after a struggle, managed to escape. He now plays Inspector Dale Smith – and therefore Tony Stamp's boss. So be careful how you treat people as you never know.... And one hit wonder Chesney Hawkes, who had a huge hit with The One and Only was apparently in some scenes with me in an episode called Photo Finish in 1991, but I'm embarrassed to say I don't remember him. That's the same with so many youngsters. When I meet them as adults they've changed so much and I love it when they jog my memory.

I often thought that when *The Bill* bandwagon arrived on location, it looked like a third rate Zippo's circus. What with the old double decker bus that acted as the canteen, wardrobe truck and Winnebagos, where the actors changed and hung out in-between scenes; this lot had all seen better days. And the toilets were always miles away from the set, usually in a car park, so as not to upset the residents. Well it can't have been very pleasant having those stuck outside your front door. And security could be an issue. There have been quite a few times when members of the public were abusive, normally accusing actors of earning far too much money. If only.

Sometimes the estates that double for the notorious Jasmine Allen could be just as dodgy so there had to be a fair amount of liaison with the locals. *The Bill* does not want to antagonise anyone. And when the show was filming in those kinds of places, the crew also had to liaise with the real police in case they were doing some low-key policing. One thing you don't want is to swamp the place with a bunch of look-a-like coppers. Once I was chatting to a uniformed copper who I assumed was on standby for guidance on police methods but told me, "Oh, no sir, I'm here for your protection."

However, most of the time people were good natured. Some kids came running over to you and would say funny things like, "My mum really fancies you." I never knew quite how to reply to that!

But some locations could simply be rather nasty. I remember once Lisa Geoghan (Polly Page) and I arrived at this horrible house which, in the story, was supposed to be where a pensioner had died. There were old newspapers everywhere, a few cats and a terrible smell. I often thought *The Bill* should be shown in 'smellavision' so the audience can get a whiff of what we had to put up with in some of those stairwells. I remarked on what a great job the props guys had done converting this place into a pig sty, only to be told that they had done hardly anything; this was how it really was. Apparently the owner had started living like this since his mother died 10 years earlier. There were dirty pots on the stove and the props guys were afraid to touch the curtains in case they disintegrated.

When the owner appeared, he had an unruly beard and the filthiest hands I have ever seen. He offered Lisa a sandwich which she politely refused.

Lisa had an aversion to cats but unfortunately this storyline called on Page and Stamp being called to a house full of them. To try to appease Lisa, the props boys brought in a few stuffed ones. Being the mischief maker I am, I couldn't resist throwing them at her from time to time but always in a caring, sharing way. The pair of us itched all day which I think in my case, served me right.

Sometimes we didn't even have the luxury of Winnebagos and had to get changed in a pub toilet. As you walked through, you couldn't win: if you didn't say hello, you were stuck up and if you did, it was a case of who does he think he is? Lovely Trudie Goodwin, who played Sergeant June Ackland, swears that she was once on the loo when a piece of paper and a pen were pushed under the door in the hope of an autograph. I always ensure I have plenty of photo postcards with me. The press office was probably thoroughly fed up with me because I got through so many of them, but fans of *The Bill* loved them and, after all, that's what they were for.

Days on set could be long and being a cheerful soul I rarely got moody but there was one time when a director's lack of respect pushed me to the edge. He had his headphones on and I presumed that he was watching the monitors where you can see what is being filmed. But when I discovered that not only was he listening to his own music during takes, he was also blatantly reading a newspaper, I saw red. I approached him and said, "I'm sorry if we are boring you but if you don't get rid of that newspaper, I will shove it up a place where the sun doesn't shine." I never saw the paper again. If there is one thing I can't stand, it is disrespectful behaviour.

The most enduring relationship I ever had on *The Bill* was with Andy Paul who played PC Dave Quinnan. On and off screen we were a great partnership and I, and Stamp, missed him terribly when he left. Andy is a top bloke. A great actor, with a tremendous eye for detail, he is also a devoted family man and just a lovely guy to be around. One thing I will add though is that I can't say I ever missed him banging on about his beloved Arsenal all the time!

I also missed Trudie Goodwin when she left in 2007 after 23 years in the series. Trudie was incredibly kind to me when I first started and continued to be a great mate. She knew it was time to leave *The Bill* when she was given a storyline involving being raped by a 14-year-old, believing that after all her character had been through, this was verging on the ridiculous. I missed Trudie a great deal when she left – she's a great actor and a lovely woman. She was hugely respected by the cast and crew on the show and she was always very supportive of me.

Looking back, my fellow actors were incredibly kind to me. I will always be grateful to Eric Richard, who played firm but fair Sergeant Bob Cryer so brilliantly. He had the ability, like me - so I've been told - to play a copper so convincingly that you really believed in him. In the early days Eric was generous enough to allow me to be noticed in scenes we shared. We shared a dressing room for a long time and we used to have a lot of good chats about life.

And Mark Wingett was such a powerful actor. His portrayal of PC Jim Carver descending into alcoholism was mesmerising and I really liked doing scenes with Mark, who is a great guy in real life. I used to have a lot of proper blokey conversations with Mark.

I always enjoyed doing scenes with the legendary Detective

Inspector Frank Burnside, played superbly by Christopher Ellison. Unlike his alter ego, Chris was anything but scary off set but sometimes he did get annoyed with me when I mucked about a little too much for his liking, asking, "Do we have to do this scene again because of him?" Fortunately, the answer was always a resounding no.

The show has had an array of wonderful female actresses over the years including Lynne Miller, who played PC Cathy Marshall, the first female character to be killed off in *The Bill*; Bernie Nolan (Sergeant Sheelagh Murphy) who proved to be just as good an actress as she is a singer; former *EastEnders* and *Footballers' Wives* star Gillian Taylforth (Sergeant Nikki Wright) who had a wicked sense of humour. And the lovely Lisa Geoghan, who was just as sweet when in civvies as her character, PC Polly Page, was.

However for me, one of the most powerful had to be Roberta Taylor. What a character she created in Inspector Gina Gold. I loved her from day one; strong, determined and a great actor. When she joined *The Bill* in 2002 it was just what the show needed. A really tough lady cop who took no prisoners. I loved our scenes together especially when Stamp was getting a roasting from Inspector Gold.

My only complaint was that I had the dressing room next door to her and Roberta smoked like a trooper. Back then it was still legal to smoke indoors. Sorry Robbie, I love you dearly, but the lack of windows and air conditioning meant the unwelcome smell of smoke regularly wafted in my direction.

But sometimes you can't get on with everyone. When Paul Usher joined as PC Des Taviner in 2001, we were filming one of his first scenes in the canteen. During a break he looked at me and said, "You don't like me do you?" I looked at him aghast. He continued, "I played Barry in *Brookside*, so that's probably why." I couldn't believe what I was hearing so I turned around and replied, "Look mate I never watched it so I don't know what you are talking about."

Now *The Bill* is filmed with only one camera which means you have to shoot a scene several times to get the different shots, unlike say *EastEnders* which is multi-cam – using several cameras at the same time. So when it came to the 'reverse shot' of the scene, I was expecting to read my lines with Paul. But he was nowhere to be found and a crew member offered to read his lines instead. "No way," I declared, "You had better get him back here." And they did. I told him, in no uncertain terms, that, "I don't know how it worked in *Brookside*, but here we support each other." After that, we kept each other at arm's length. I don't think he was deliberately being awkward; it was simply what he was used to. I'm pleased to say he soon got used to the way things were done at *The Bill*.

And despite being a brilliant on screen double act, Paul and Jeff Stewart, who played PC Reg Hollis didn't get on that well. Jeff was a comic genius but you had to be patient to get those amusing gems. It was a bit like a comic's straight man, constantly feeding him the lines. But Paul wasn't interested in being Jeff's comic feed, which I suppose is fair enough. Jeff and Paul's on screen relationship made great telly, and if I'm honest I guess I was a bit jealous of him because Tony Stamp was Reg Hollis's sidekick for a while and I would have loved some of the great lines Paul got as Des Taviner in his scenes with Jeff.

Even *The Bill* has been hit by tragedy. One of the saddest moments during my tenure has to be when Kevin Lloyd, who played DC Alfred 'Tosh' Lines, died in 1998. We had become good mates and would often holiday together with our families in Devon. He and his family had a caravan in Salcombe, Devon and we met up with them two or three times over the years and we shared some fantastic holidays. My kids, Matthew and Laura got on really well with Kevin's, especially Poppy, who now works in the casting department of *The Bill* and James, who played PC Steve Hunter from 2004 to 2006.

When Kevin joined in 1988, we all thought it was perfect casting. Kevin had a good track record with a string of television appearances in shows like *Coronation Street,* in which he'd played nightclub owner Don Watkins, *Auf Wiedersehen, Pet* and John Sullivan's sitcom *Dear John* in which he played ageing rock star Ricky Fortune. He also had a solid theatre background including a spell at the Liverpool Everyman where he worked with luminaries such as Bill Nighy, Pete Postlethwaite and Julie Walters.

Tosh was just what CID needed. He brought a softer, more humane side to CID, counterbalancing beautifully the likes of hardman DI Frank Burnside (Christopher Ellison). Like a UK version of Columbo, his scruffy rain mac became his trademark.

Both the character of Tosh and Kevin himself, who was a great ensemble actor, easily slotted in. Whether Tosh was talking to his snouts or inadvisably eating yet another fry up, he was utterly believable.

I liked Kevin a lot. He was an incredibly likeable person yet as an actor he was frustrated and he shouldn't have been. He was enormously talented but like me he wanted to be the lead all the time, but being in a show like *The Bill* meant that was never going to happen because *The Bill* is such an ensemble show.

Things began to go horribly wrong in Kevin's life. He was insistent on travelling back to the family home in Derbyshire nearly every night. He and his wife Lesley had six children and understandably, he didn't like being away from them. During the two-hour train journey, he would join the drinking club in the bar, to ease the strain of what was already a demanding schedule. Something had to give.

Despite being friends, Kevin would sometimes have a dig at me. It would annoy him that at charity functions I was always asked to compere the auctions. Sadly, it was more to do with him being merry rather than differences in our ability. He would imply that as he was a CID character, he outranked me. This was something many of the regulars in *The Bill* actually believed and I would have to remind them that it wasn't real and that screen rank had no bearing on or off set.

As the drink started to affect Kevin's performance, his fellow actors rallied round. One day we were sat in the Winnebago and he was in tears as he was having real trouble with his lines. Not for the first time Chris Ellison came to his aid, "Kevin, don't worry about that line. I think it would make more sense if I or Graham said it." Chris' generosity towards his fellow actors personified *The Bill* and shows what a good actor Chris is, and as I've said before, nothing like hard man Burnside in real-life.

But Kevin was in denial and when his marriage broke up, his life began spiralling out of control. *The Bill* management had tried to help by paying for him to go into rehab several times but nothing worked.

His problems escalated and eventually, after putting up with his lateness, his inability to always remember his lines and his habit of wandering off without telling anyone where he was going, for long enough the bosses were left with little option and he was sacked.

Kevin died on 2nd May 1998, a week after his dismissal. He was just 49. He had been in a clinic but had left and had apparently had started drinking again. Six days later he was admitted to hospital in Burton-on-Trent where he died. I was at work when I heard the news. Ironically enough I was filming a six-part story featuring Stamp running over a pedestrian which meant I was already in an emotional state, as the story was quite draining.

The news of Kevin's death was a terrible blow. The building was sombre and although we tried as hard as we could, none of the cast or crew could concentrate. So I asked the director if we could stop to give everyone a chance to get their head around it. And we all had a group hug. None of us were surprised but everyone felt it was an awful waste. Kevin had written a book called *The Man Who Loved Too Much,* which I think was a fitting title.

# CHAPTER SEVEN

# Case Files

A biography on *The Bill* website described my former alter ego as follows: 'PC Tony Stamp, Serial number: 595 remains utterly contented to be a PC, as long as he doesn't have to hand the keys over to some young pretender. He may well be institutionalised, but he hasn't become cynical or embittered; he genuinely enjoys being part of London's biggest gang, and the younger members of the team completely respect him for that.' Blunt but true. I think you could probably have said pretty much the same about Graham Cole, especially as in the end I was the longest serving cast member in *The Bill*, beating Trudie Goodwin by just a year.

According to *The Bill* archive, Tony Stamp was born in Slough and joined the police as a teenager. After a few years in the Thames Valley police, he transferred to the Metropolitan police, convinced it would be more exciting. And he was right.

Of course I thought PC Tony Stamp was one of the most important characters in *The Bill* but then I would wouldn't I? Seen as kind and honest, he was regarded as a copper's copper, by both the public and the police alike, which I took as a huge compliment both to myself and the writers. Over that period of 25 years I appeared in roughly 1,000 episodes out of over 2,000. Not bad for a character originally conceived as a mute extra.

I remember appearing on ITV1's *This Morning* a few years ago, along with Kevin Lloyd and we were asked which other character you would like to play in *The Bill*. Kevin immediately answered, "DI Frank Burnside," but I couldn't imagine playing anyone else other than PC Stamp. He might not have been the most dynamic police officer but I know if I was burgled, I would want someone like Stamp on the case. He actually looked as if he cared enough to do something about it.

People often asked me why he never became a sergeant. Well, he always thought he was still one of the lads but of course, he wasn't. But he was the area car boy which he loved. He never had a desire to move into CID, although he did the odd bit of undercover work, even getting behind the wheel as an HGV driver. What so many people fail to realise is that CID are not above uniform. It is a bit like the difference between a GP and a hospital doctor. One is a jack of all trades while the other has chosen to specialise but, unless they are a consultant, the latter is not above the former. In a similar way, CID has squads like murder and robbery, who specialise in a particular area. But just because they are in plain clothes, does not automatically make them above the bobbies on the beat. And anyway, when June Ackland was promoted to Sergeant, it seemed the writers didn't know what to do with her after that.

Stamp simply loved being on the frontline of policing and meeting the public. And was not afraid to stand up for what's right, a quality I can strongly empathise with. And sometimes it costs. He'd been beaten up more times than I care to remember, shot at, stabbed and even had fridges thrown at him, but admirably he still came back for more.

Over the years Stamp was given some great lines by the writers. And I loved delivering them with all my might. There's a storyline involving a group of teenagers with learning difficulties who are being targeted by a bully. Stamp has been called back to their flat for the umpteenth time and by now is really cheesed off. So he gets hold of the perpetrator by the scruff of the neck, bangs him up against the wall and says, "In the first place you are obstructing a officer in the course of his duty and secondly, why don't you pick on someone your own size if that is biologically possible." Great stuff.

Another time Stamp and PC Reg Hollis are in an artist's flat and he and Hollis are bonding over avant garde film maker Jean Luc Godard. Stamp is half listening to what he thinks is a load of old cobblers. So when the artist asks him if he is a fan, he replies, "I myself am a great fan of *Die Hard* and you're nicked."

One of the funniest lines I ever had was at the end of an episode called Hers, in 1996. Stamp and PC Polly Page (Lisa Geoghan) are investigating the case of an undertaker who has lost his hearse, which contains the body of a thief. In keeping with the black humour of the story, my final line is, "A hearse, a hearse. My kingdom for a hearse." Delivered, on my part, with relish.

Sometimes I liked to have a little input of my own. Once I was filming an episode outside Wimbledon Theatre and had to arrest an Elvis impersonator who had chained himself to a parking meter. He was aptly dressed in the whole white suit regalia and out of his head on something. So on the third take, Stamp can't resist asking him if he is, "'All Shook Up' and does he fancy, 'A Little Less Conversation.'" As I left the scene, I was singing, "A little more love, a little less conversation...." which I added. I was well chuffed when they left it in.

For various reasons, you could sometimes end up with a script which was written for a specific character who is now no longer available, maybe because the actor was ill. So with the stroke of a Tippex pen, PC Roger Valentine's lines suddenly become PC Tony Stamp's, for example. It might not read like Stamp on the page but my job was to make it sound like him when filming.

I did question the management's plans for Stamp and sometimes had to put my foot down. They were planning to marry him off but I didn't feel it was right. He had his fair share of dalliances and even proposes to a nurse called Julie who replies, "I'll marry you but not the force." The next day he explains to Sergeant Cryer (Eric Richard) his dilemma. "I love her and want to marry her but I want to be a copper too." The wise Sergeant's response is spot on when he says, "But you're a copper aren't you?" And that's just it. He's married to the job. Appropriately, that was the name of the episode, which was written by Roger Leach, who also played Sergeant Tom Penny. Anyway, in the end she turns him down flat so he doesn't have to wrestle with his conscience after all.

And hard as he tried, Stamp never had much luck in the love department. The unlucky loser had a go at video dating, speed dating and in one episode, even hires an escort for the evening to pretend to be his girlfriend, only to be greeted by a colleague, PC Amber Johanssen, played by the delightful Myfanwy Waring, who is doing a spot of moonlighting. Stamp works it to his advantage and promises not to tell the senior officers if she keeps up the charade. Typically, the little minx exploits the role and uses Stamp to wine and dine her. However, he later gets his own back by dedicating a karaoke version of the Carly Simon classic You're So Vain to her. Both Myfanwy and I relished these slightly out of character scenarios for Johanssen and Stamp. And I couldn't resist giving my all when it came to the singing scene. But as always, Stamp is brought down to earth with a bump and truly devastated when he discovers that another girlfriend, Mae Santos, is part of an immigration racket.

Still he lived in hope and for me, being a happily married man, it was far more of a challenge to play someone whose circumstances were polar opposite to mine. You don't come into the acting profession to play yourself. Stamp was a single man. I used to imagine his bachelor pad having a state of the art TV and sound system, a microwave and that's about it. I always thought he should also have a flash motor but the producers seemed reluctant to grant my wish.

Another time I was a little disappointed when a juicy storyline involving Stamp being stabbed and seriously wounded was abandoned because the producers felt it was too shocking for a family audience. I thought it should have been shown so viewers were reminded of the dangers policemen face on a daily basis while patrolling the streets. Later they had a change of heart but decided PC Dave Quinnan (Andrew Paul) should be on the receiving end instead.

I would have been perfectly happy to do bedroom scenes if necessary but I don't think viewers wanted to see Stamp from that perspective. The nearest he ever got to getting his kit off in front of a lady was in an episode called That Ol' Mullarkey which focused on Stamp's birthday. He's called to the house of an attractive young woman who claims she has been attacked. But there are bars on the windows and she is actually planning to seduce him. Over the radio come the voices of his colleagues, urging him to get back to Sun Hill as they are ready to start celebrating. On hearing this, the deranged lady accidentally on purpose spills red wine on his white shirt, forcing him to take it off. She ventures into the bathroom, saying she is going to put it into soak but when he enters she is actually in the bath, ready and waiting. Luckily PC Reg Hollis, of all people, comes to the rescue, along with the Fire Brigade to put out the blaze she has deliberately started. I received a letter about the episode but not complimenting me on the wonderful drama I had created. Instead it was a thank you for going back and saving the budgie.

In 1996 *The Bill* celebrated its 999th episode. Called Spill, it was a one-hour special focusing on trying to avert a disaster when a chemical tanker overturns near a London Underground station. It was a clever scenario as it involved all three emergency services: police, fire brigade and ambulance. We began filming at the Woolwich Arsenal late afternoon and didn't finish until the early hours. And it was the middle of January so absolutely freezing. During a break in filming, a kind old lady invited me in for a cup of tea which I was more than happy to accept.

I was often mistaken for a real copper and on this occasion a van pulled over and started to ask me for directions. He didn't have a clue who I was and I couldn't help so he drove off mumbling about "unhelpful coppers." Another time I was at a set of traffic lights when a car pulled up beside me. The music was blaring and four young lads were singing along when they suddenly spotted me and all four put their seat belts on.

In Spill the firemen are concerned about chemical contamination so we all have to be hosed down. The water was ice cold but at least the male members of the cast could wear wet suits under their uniform. Poor old Lisa Geoghan (PC Polly Page) couldn't because she was wearing a skirt.

The first time Stamp stares death in the face is in 1993 in an episode called Short Straw. Nula Conwell, who played DC Viv Martella, had decided to leave so the producers devised a dramatically permanent exit. The storyline involved Martella getting on the wrong side of DI Frank Burnside, not for the first time, and being excluded from a CID operation against a group of armed robbers. She commandeers Stamp to help her with a routine enquiry about a handbag snatcher. The pair spot a parked van and thinking nothing of it, Martella approaches the driver. Shockingly, he points a double barrel shotgun in her face and shoots her dead, before shooting Stamp, as he dives for cover. Though thankfully, for both Stamp and myself, not fatally. I wasn't ready to go just yet. The episode was a huge ratings winner but I was sad to see Nula go.

When Paul Marquess took over the reins as executive producer in 2002, he told me he was planning a six-part storyline involving Stamp being accused of being a paedophile. I think my reaction surprised him. It sounded as if he was expecting me to be anti but I couldn't be more positive. Here was a story that would play very much against type for good ol' reliable PC Stamp and, as an actor, I could really get my teeth into.

The episodes turned out to be even better than I could ever have hoped. After being nominated as Community Bobby of the Year, Stamp is accused of indecently assaulting a lad called Lee Dwyer and suspended. His colleagues are shocked but inevitably some believe there is no smoke without fire. Stamp's world collapses and he is a broken man. The scenes were tough but enormously rewarding to play as I love having pages and pages of dialogue and being put through the emotional ringer. All the scenes were pretty harrowing but the one where he discovers 'Ponce' painted on the front of his house is probably the toughest. Stamp hears over the radio that his colleagues are dealing with a disturbance and recognises the address as his. When he arrives home, a crowd have gathered outside and start shouting abuse at him. I am lucky enough not to need a tear stick to help me cry on camera. I knew the character so well that as I was filming I could really feel Stamp's pain that the tears flowed easily. And on the way home, for the first time in all my years on *The Bill*, I had to pull over and have another cry. It's not that often that a storyline gets to you that deeply but this one certainly did at the time and I really felt Stamp's sadness.

Finally Stamp is cleared; turns out it's the young lad's own father who has been abusing him, but understandably the whole affair leaves a bitter taste in his mouth. And he takes it out on one of his oldest colleagues, DC Jim Carver, who he feels hasn't been supportive enough. Dramatically he tells him, "Our paths needn't ever cross again but if they do, ignore me because as far as I'm concerned, you're dead." A hard line to deliver to a friend both on and off screen. Thankfully, salt of the earth Inspector Gina Gold (Roberta Taylor) never believed a word of it. And nor did quite a few viewers. I had some lovely letters saying, "We knew it wasn't you."

When, in 2003, I heard that *The Bill* was going to do a live episode I was beside myself with excitement. It had been years since I had done any theatre and I was so up for the challenge. The episode revolves around DC Juliet Becker, played by the lovely Rae Baker, being taken hostage and Sun Hill's efforts to free her from a mad man. Unfortunately we don't succeed and she is fatally stabbed.

Seeing that out of the cast I probably had the most experience of live theatre, I foolishly thought I would have a bigger role but it was not to be. I was just one of the uniformed bobbies running around in the background, with the odd line thrown in.

The evening of 30th October 2003, just five minutes before we went live, while some other cast members were being sick and trying to calm their nerves, I was chatting in the canteen with Cherry and some friends who had come to watch this momentous occasion.

If viewers could see the chaos that surrounded us during the broadcast, they would have been hysterical with laughter. People were pulling cables all over the place, moving lights and sound equipment just a few feet from the action. I loved every minute of it and thought the crew were magnificent to be able to pull off something so technically difficult. They deserved a BAFTA, which *The Bill* finally won in 2009, and it was superb to be a part of television history.

The experiment was so successful that *The Bill* did it again in September 2005 which coincided with ITV celebrating its 50th anniversary. The episode involves a siege situation when a grief stricken father holds a group of officers and civilians hostage upstairs in CID. I didn't have much to do in that one either but my daughter Laura, who has been to drama school, plays Miss Canley, the carnival queen who is escorted by the Mayor. Clearly following in her mother's footsteps as a beauty queen, I thought she was great but I would say that wouldn't I?

Trudie Goodwin and I had worked together for nearly 20 years when, in 2003, the powers that be decided we should have a romantic interlude. That storyline did surprise me a little because Stamp had always had a soft spot for PC Polly Page (Lisa Geoghan). And only the year before, Stamp had made a pass at June Ackland and got a slap in the face for his trouble. After that incident I got lots of little old ladies coming up to me and saying, "June shouldn't have done that. We still love you." One time Cherry was with me and after half an hour of witnessing me being constantly accosted, gave up on our shopping trip and retreated to the car to wait for me.

Trudie and I were and are great friends and I knew she was anxious about filming our first kiss. The morning of the shoot, I saw her in make-up and she looked really nervous. So I went over, gently pulled her head back, and gave her a great big smacker. "Now, Trudie, it couldn't be any worse than that could it?" And it wasn't. Even though it was a bit like kissing your sister.

I particularly enjoyed the 2005 episode that briefly introduced Stamp's father. Veteran actor John Woodvine, who had played Joe Jacobs in *Emmerdale,* was simply brilliant as Norman Stamp. We also discover in that story that Stamp has a sister Jacquie, played by the lovely Pauline Whittaker, who contacts her brother to alert him of their dad's declining health. Stamp always believed that his father did not approve of his job and his father's brusque dismissal of his son's affection and verbal abuse seemed to support that. To get right inside Stamp's head, I built up a back story which had Norman as a regimental sergeant major who was away a lot and I drew on my own loneliness as a child to portray Stamp's inner conflicts over his father. Struggling to pay Norman's care home fees, I was proud of my alter ego, who was moonlighting as a taxi driver. Sadly his father grows weaker and dies in hospital but thankfully, not before the two make their peace. And I was delighted when Stamp discovers that his father was proud of him all along, after his sister shows him a scrapbook his father kept, full of newspaper cuttings about his son. The storyline reminded me a little of my own Dad, although he was always supportive if somewhat bewildered by what his son was up to.

Many a time my big gob got me into trouble on set. In 2004 Stamp was DS Jim Carver's best man when he married Sergeant June Ackland. It was a bit of a ménage a trios because of Stamp and Ackland's previous fling. We were filming at a beautiful stately home and I thought the speech was very dull and there wasn't even a comical reference to the fact that Stamp had, only a few months earlier, run Ackland over. Only in soap land. The wonderful Roberta Taylor (Inspector Gina Gold) was horrified at how boring it was but I explained I had mentioned it to the producer but she wasn't budging. By now I was delivering the best man's speech for the 18th time, as it involved a long, complex tracking shot. So to liven things up for the next take, I delivered a slightly amended version, "I am really sorry for knocking you over, causing you to lose your spleen, but I understand sex is a lot better." Well the room erupted but boy was I in trouble.

The next day, after watching the rushes (the raw filmed footage), the series producer, Claire Phillips, hauled me into her office. "Graham, I don't think you take this job very seriously do you? I watched the rushes and was very upset by what I saw." I'm afraid I couldn't help myself and replied, "Then don't watch the rushes."

I then checked with the director and she was quite happy.

So I went to see Paul Marquess, who, incidentally, had written the episode. Gravely, I offered my resignation, "I think we have a problem here and if you want me to go, I will." But he too was cool and wouldn't hear of it. The thing about rushes is that they are full of bloopers and mistakes and that's why they are carefully screened; the best take is singled out to be used while the rest end up on the cutting room floor or occasionally on shows like Denis Norden's *It'll Be Alright on the Night.*

Another favourite episode of mine is when Andy Paul and I had to bear our bottoms. Stamp tells the relief that he has a bet on with the rival Barton Street station that Sun Hill can nick more villains than them during a shift. What he doesn't tell his colleagues is that there's a forfeit. The losers have to do the conga in the nude at a forthcoming party. The producer, Brenda Ennis, explained that we would be shooting at Tooting Police Station's section house and warned that our backsides would be on display. Nude scenes are never pleasant at the best of times and I had only ever been nude once before, during my theatrical career. It was in a play called *Boys in the Band* and my character had to exit out of the bathroom and streak across the stage to the bedroom.

No points for guessing that Sun Hill lost the bet. It was the last shot of the day and Stamp and Quinnan had to come out of the men's toilets and walk away from the camera, starkers. Derek Cotty, the red unit's smashing production manager, came into the Winnebago, offering us a bottle of scotch as Dutch courage. But Andy and I declined. We preferred to wait until the shot was in the can.

We had been led to believe that only a few cast members would be around but when we went on set, there were an additional 45 extras also in our eye line. Andy immediately went to elaborate measures to cover up his manhood, using a cricket box and tape whereas I was past caring. We did the shot and were looking forward to a drop of scotch when we got back to the Winnebago. I reckon Mr Cotty, who was known to be frugal with his budget, had nabbed the bottle back!

And it was the same Mr Cotty who assured me that there was no danger of catching Weil's Disease when I waded into the River Wandle after a suspect. "The water's fine Graham. I've just checked it." I still wasn't convinced. "The thing is Derek, today is Tuesday, by Thursday, when we film the scene, today's water will be half way to France." I did it though. That's the job.

I was injured a few times on *The Bill* but ironically the one that still gives me the odd twinge didn't happen in the area car but in Sun Hill's Custody Suite. In this particular scene Stamp is being a naughty boy by taking a wee in one of the cells, which is strictly against the rules. PC Norika Datta (Seeta Indrani) is bringing in a prisoner when he threatens her with a knife. Stamp is supposed to take his boots off, so the villain won't hear him, and creep up behind him. We rehearsed it a couple of times and then went for a take. I now took my shoes off, and was in my socks, so unfortunately, when I went to grab him, I slipped. We were both in the air and I thought he is only a slight lad, about 18, so if I land on him I am going to do some real damage so I pushed him away from me. Unfortunately I landed on my hip but we carried on

Cherry and I on our wedding day - I was glad when she finally turned up.

How did I manage to get so much confetti on my head? Doesn't Cherry look beautiful!

With my heroes Vincent Price and Peter Cushing- they were scary on-screen but real gentleman off.

Fulfilling my King Rat's duties with
Nicholas Parsons.

At the Variety Club awards with
David Gower.

He's behind you....as Melkur in Doctor Who.

26th January 1982

Dear Graham,

Thank you again for your hard work and patience during the studios for the 'Dr. Who' story "Earthshock."

I am sure that the costumes were extremely uncomfortable to wear. However, they have made you all the most spectacular Cybermen that have ever appeared in the series.

We are now editing the programme and it promises to be a very exciting story.

Once more, congratulations on your endurance. I hope that we can work together again.

Best wishes,

(Peter Grimwade)

Graham Cole,
Ivor Kimmel Casting Agency.

Suffering for my art...

Can you tell it's me?

With my pride and joy - Sierra One.

An early publicity shot for The Bill.

In my favourite role - as a dad.

Trying to swap pens with Linda Lusardi.

With Noel Edmonds - who was very generous with his helicopter.

With the kids and Cherry in Australia in 1994.

Handcuffed for the press but by Aussie police officers.

The old Bill - some of the cast larking around on set in the early 1990s.

Sun Hill's finest circa 1999 - how many can you name?

With Tony Booth and Liz Smith.

With Zig and Zag.

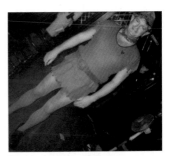

The Wild Bunch.

Working for the elf service...

Top days for The Bill - winning a National Television Award in 1996, beating Band of Gold and Heartbeat.

PCs Stamp and Valentine (John Bowler) in action.

Larking around with Sam Callis
(Sergeant Callum Stone).

Working with two greats: Ron Moody and Mollie Sugden in the
glamour setting of Croydon Market.

Stamp on trial. Getting the Flying Squad tie
on TV earned a charity £100.

You're nicked...Stamp the thief taker.

Constable Stamp in 2009

filming. Afterwards I was taken off to see a doctor and I'd badly bruised my leg and had x-rays taken to make sure nothing was broken but to this day it still aches from time to time.

And then there was the time I was bitten on the foot by some creature that to this day no one has ever been able to identify. We were filming in a warehouse and all of a sudden I felt something bite me. Next thing I knew my foot started swelling up like a balloon and throbbing. Despite my discomfort, once again the show must go on and only after three takes was I allowed to be taken off to hospital where I was given an antihistamine injection. Several crew were also bitten but none of us ever found out what it was. But it must have had an almighty pair of gnashers as it had managed to bite through a police regulation boot.

On another occasion it was a colleague who was on the receiving end of an accidental right hook during a punch up scene. Cyril Nri played Superintendent Adam Okaro and as boss of Sun Hill, he rarely got involved in stunts. But in this particular episode, he was in the thick of it. Being a bit more experienced I suggested to the director that he should not do the scene too many times as someone would get hurt. Of course he didn't listen to me and someone did get landed one and it was Cyril. He had been fighting with a stuntman when a punch caught him right on the mouth and one of his crowns was knocked out. Poor Cyril, a smashing chap and a very good actor, had to take four days off.

Whenever a cast regular leaves *The Bill* there is a stampede to get their dressing room if it is better than yours. When I heard a particularly desirable space was vacant, I asked the management if I could have it. But it was too late, Cyril had got there first. I wonder who got mine when I left....

Proud as I was of Stamp's iconic status, even I was surprised at the effect he has not only on members of the public but fellow actors too. A group of kids were giving Stamp the run-around and when we stopped for a break, one of them remarked, "My mum would kill me if she thought I was beating up PC Stamp." Even seasoned actors seem to melt in his presence. When Lisa Geoghan (PC Polly Page) joined the show, she couldn't contain her excitement at being out on the beat with PC Stamp. "I'm so used to seeing you on the telly; I can't believe I am really out on the streets with PC Stamp." And George Rossi, who played DC Duncan Lennox, was struck dumb when he had to open the door to PC Stamp.

Even PC Stamp - or was it Graham Cole - had the odd stalker. One was particularly persistent. I was filming in Croydon when I spotted her. The security guys had told her where our location was just to get rid of her. My heart sank; this wasn't the first time she had hung around. She was in her 20s and nice enough, just a bit weird. She was decked out in high heels and every time I moved off set, I could hear the clip clop of those stilettos behind me. When we broke for lunch, I said "Hello," and quickly darted into the Winnebago, hoping she would get the message and leave. But she wasn't going anywhere and simply stood outside waiting for me to reappear. I didn't like the idea of her following me off set so when I finished filming my bit, I got changed as quickly as I could and made a run for it. I had parked my car about 10 minutes away at the Fairfield Halls but instead of going through the underpass, to save time, I risked life and limb by nipping across the dual carriageway. After paying at the machine, I headed for the car, convinced I had out witted her. So imagine my astonishment when there she was, bold as brass, standing in front of my car.

Another time I was parked at *The Bill* base and clocked her hanging around the building again. I enlisted production managers Derek Cotty and Brian Heard to help me make my escape as I was concerned she would try to throw herself in front of the car. As I exited the car park, in my rear view mirror I could see Brian constraining her in a bear hug, legs kicking wildly as she tried to break free and pursue me.

When a new character joined *The Bill*, I liked to decide for myself whether Stamp was going to like them or not. He really took to PC Roger Valentine, as did I to the actor John Bowler, who plays him. But Stamp was never too keen on DCI Jack Meadows (Simon Rouse). I like Simon although I've never been that close to him like I was and still am to John.

We used to have a lot of fun on set and I always enjoyed working with Jeff Stewart (PC Reg Hollis). We were once doing a scene involving Hollis and Stamp chasing some kids through a deserted factory. It was a good two and a half minutes and with all the gear on, it was heavy going. In the scene we had to catch up with these toe rags, pin one of them to the floor and read him his rights: "You do not have to say anything but if you do, it may harm your defence." The usual spiel. By the third take we were both shattered. So when we got this kid on the ground, neither of us was firing on all cylinders. Suddenly this kid's leg kicks out and accidentally catches Jeff in the unmentionables. Jeff is obviously in pain but despite hobbling off, no one shouts, "Cut," so the camera keeps rolling. And I carry on with the scene; cuff the kid and read him his rights. I can see Jeff out of the corner of my eye and he is creased up in pain but being an old pro he struggles back on and helps me lift the kid up. Finally after what felt like an eternity, the director shouts "Cut!" No one seemed to have noticed Jeff's misfortune. I tried to explain but for a solid 20 minutes, I couldn't stop laughing. And Jeff being battered for real was the take they used.

In the 1991 episode Skeletons, Hollis and Stamp think they have stumbled across the lair of a modern day Jack the Ripper when they are called to a deserted flat full of skeletons. The atmosphere is sombre until someone points out that they are actually made of plastic and used by medical students. As usual I couldn't resist mucking about. Firstly I told Jeff that he should keep moving in case anyone thought he was one of the skeletons. And then I kept singing Dem Bones, Dem Bones. Then the crew got in on the act by laying one skeleton on top of the other, as you do. I thought it was funny but Jeff wasn't amused.

But then Jeff rarely laughed on set. But when he did he was a real giggler. One time we were doing a canteen scene and sitting at one of the tables. The director kept asking me to get closer and closer to him so that in the end I looked like some kind of giant squeezing the life out of this tiny man. As Jeff realised how ridiculous we must look, he burst out laughing. He really was a comic genius. Another time he was sitting in the canteen delivering his lines and eating yoghurt with a fork. For no reason other than he knew it was funny.

I loved working with Jeff and was very upset over the way he left *The Bill*. He had joined the show around the same time as me and made PC Reg Hollis one of *The Bill*'s most popular characters. But sometimes he was not the easiest actor to work with but I think it was because he really cared. If his call time was 7.30am, he would turn up exactly then but still needed to take a shower, shave and have some breakfast instead of heading straight for make-up. He had already been warned about being late and had this annoying habit of turning up on set in a dressing gown, without his full uniform, while we were all suited and booted. We would rehearse, be ready for a take and only then would he take off the gown, and start putting on his boots and tunic. This delayed filming no end. And between takes he would leave the set and wander around the building, once again in his dressing gown along with a pair of slippers with the runners desperately trying to find him.

I was with him on set the day it all came to a head but ironically he was standing up for another actress. They were filming one of those dreadful parade scenes and the actress in question had missed a note the director had given her so was being given a gentle reprimand and reminded of what he wanted her to do. For some reason Jeff stepped in and a row ensued between him and the director. When he told Jeff to mind his own business, he saw red and got up to leave. Storming out, he kicked the door open, nearly pushing the production assistant through it as he brushed past and promptly disappeared. Later he was given yet another warning rather than the sack so obviously thought everything was hunky dory.

But his unpredictable behaviour put the management in a difficult position. So when the producers, script editors and writers gathered for their monthly meeting, it was decided the end was nigh for PC Reg Hollis and began planning a two-part leaving episode. The news, unsurprisingly, sent Jeff over the edge as *The Bill* was his life. No one other than Jeff truly knows what went on in his dressing room shortly afterward but I later heard that he rang security to say there was blood everywhere. The unwitting security guy said he would bring a cloth but Jeff replied, "You will need something bigger." So the poor bloke had no idea what Jeff meant until he entered his dressing room and was confronted with blood everywhere.

Jeff then started running up and down the corridor, dripping blood and shouting, "I am *The Bill*!" As they waited for an ambulance, the producers tried to calm him down but he kept screaming that they were all guilty of betraying him. Fortunately, Bruce Byron, a terrific actor and a thoroughly nice bloke who plays DC Terry Perkins, happened to be around and turned out to be the only person who could get close to him and calm him down. Jeff was taken to hospital and a couple of girls from the press office accompanied him to the hospital and stayed with him until he was released. Fortunately his injuries weren't too serious, but he didn't come back to work.

All the cast were shocked and rallied round. Simon Rouse (DCI Jack Meadows), Andrew Lancel (DI Neil Manson) and I all rang him soon after and left messages but he hasn't called back. I imagine seeing any of us was too painful as we were, at that time, all still in the show. I don't know whether it was a cry for help but I do know that I miss him and wish him well. And I dearly hope that now I too am no longer there, he will be able to return one of those calls.

Now that I was a regular on *The Bill*, and the proud dad of two children, Cherry and I felt it was time to buy somewhere bigger. House hunting with me drove Cherry mad. We viewed over 200 properties before we found one. I think some of Tony Stamp's thoughts must have rubbed off on me as I kept annoyingly pointing out security risks. We finally settled on a house in Keston, Kent. It wasn't Cherry's favourite; she had liked another house on a posh road in Beckenham, Kent but I have always been cautious with money and felt it was too expensive. Hindsight is a wonderful thing and if I had known how long I would be in *The Bill*, I would have snapped it up. I don't think Cherry has ever forgiven me but my son Matthew said he was glad we didn't buy it as the whole set up reminded him of that film, *The Stepford Wives*.

I finally got an agent when *The Bill* reverted back to the one-hour format in 1998. I chose Jan Evans when I saw how well she represented Huw Higginson, who played PC George Garfield, during a dispute with the management over pay. And she had a strong theatrical background which I liked.

Battle commenced over revised contracts for the one hours. Now in long-running series like *The Bill* your salary is also determined by how many episodes you appear in per year. So the cast and their respective agents were all sent a letter explaining that *The Bill* would now be two one-hour episodes a week. Fine. But what wasn't fine was the next bit, 'As there are three commercial breaks per episode, you will get one payment for being in part one; two payments for also being in part two and if you appeared in all three parts, you will receive two payments.' What?

No way were we accepting that. We had been producing an hour and a half of television a week and if you were in both parts of a half-hour episode, you got two payments so it was only fair that if you were now in three, you should be paid for three. Negotiations went on for six or seven months and there were a few dirty tricks along the way including damaging headlines in the tabloid press, "Bill cast ask for double wages." At one stage a suit came down to Merton from ITV for a face to face meeting with the cast. With the actors' union Equity behind us common sense prevailed and we won in the end.

# CHAPTER EIGHT

# Sierra One

I never dreamt that I would end up being paid for two of my biggest passions in life, acting and driving. Playing the area car driver in *The Bill* was both a privilege and a pleasure. I never tired of zooming around the streets of London with the blues and twos on. Alas the show is not allowed to turn the sirens on during filming so the sound is dubbed on afterwards. But you get the picture.

PC Stamp's pride and joy was Sierra One. Behind the wheel he was king of the road. I'm sure his favourite TV programme was *Top Gear*. But I'm not sure whether he's a Jeremy, a Richard or a James. Whenever I was doing a canteen scene, where Stamp was required to be reading a paper or periodical, I always ensured it was a copy of a motoring magazine. I myself usually had a copy of *The Reader's Digest* about my person to fill any breaks in filming, stuffed in one of Stamp's many uniform pockets or pouches and easy to put down when required.

Sierra One comes in two versions. For exterior shots it's an automatic but they use a manual when filming inside the car. That manual version is also a stretch model in order to accommodate all the camera gear. So along with having to remember your lines and where you were going, you also had to remember not to use your left leg in the first shot when shooting the exterior. But use it in the second shot, when shooting the interior, as you now have to change gear. At first it was very confusing but I liked to think I got it down to a fine art. However, you could never anticipate what might happen out on the open road.

My great pal Andy Paul (PC Dave Quinnan) was President of the White Knuckle Brigade when he was sitting beside me in Sierra One. The paler he turned, the faster I would go. So it didn't take much to have him quaking in his boots. However, one near miss gave me a hell of a fright too. In this episode, a burning car has been reported on the Jasmine Allen estate, where else? The vehicle was carefully positioned on a large piece of concrete. So we did the approach shot, filming the inside of the car when Stamp and PC Dave Quinnan spot the juvenile delinquents, who set fire to it. And then swap to the automatic model for the exterior shot.

Sierra One had previously been on some muddy terrain so when I drove up onto the concrete slab, the car alarmingly went into a slide and began heading for the burning vehicle. Luckily I managed to turn the wheel, controlling the skid and ensuring it went sailing past. The only damage done was a cracked wing mirror. So, as I am sitting there, feeling quite pleased with myself, having perfectly executed a text book manoeuvre, Andy quietly asks, "Can we please move now?" Only then did I realise that the car was getting quite hot and Andy's face was turning a deep shade of scarlet. As I looked around, I saw that the fire was still burning and Sierra One, along with Andy's ears, was a little too close for comfort. I swiftly moved.

With driving being so vital to the role of Stamp, I regularly attended driving courses at the Metropolitan Police Training Headquarters in Hendon to ensure, as much as possible, that I knew what I was doing. They have been good to me at Hendon over the years. And I have been lucky enough to have been allowed on the skid pad many times. I loved skidding or should it be kidding around and I like to think that my driving skills improved. There's no doubt that I drove differently when I was playing Stamp. Certainly I went a lot faster and maybe took a few more risks than I normally would.

Any episode involving driving was a winner with me. Instant Response has a 16-minute car chase, which, in 1994, was the longest ever recorded on British television. I am not sure if that record still stands but it still remains an exciting ride for the viewers. And 16 minutes is a long time on any TV show but in an episode of *The Bill* it was almost a lifetime. It took six months to film as the weather kept changing so dramatically, from sunny one day to snowing the next. There was one hair-raising moment during shooting. I was in Sierra One and about three or four cars behind the stunt driver who was deliberately heading for a pile of pallets which he was going to crash into. Suddenly I spotted a real motor cyclist coming round the corner. Thankfully I had been trained to be aware of all eventualities and thank goodness I had already seen the motorbike; otherwise I would have ploughed straight into him.

Final Drive from 1996 is a blinder. Stamp returns to the police driving school at Hendon to learn front wheel drive skills. Having earlier been upset by comments about his age, he is delighted to nab a date with PC Jacqui Sommer, whom he meets at Hendon. Of course, as always with unlucky in love Stamp, this romance doesn't go anywhere and he is further upset by rumours sneaky PC Reg Hollis is spreading back at Sun Hill that his advanced driving skills are being reassessed. Having none of it Stamp vows to get his own back and is awarded Class One driver status in his final drive.

The Squad (2000) is a good one when Stamp is seconded to the flying squad as one of their drivers. The team are shadowing a suspect who enters a bank with an unidentified man. The squad quickly identify him as the bank's manager and ascertain that his family are being held hostage. The alarm goes off in the bank and despite Stamp's best efforts, he manages to lose both the getaway car and the vehicle with the family in it. But Stamp makes amends when he later rescues the family.

Luckily car stunts didn't go wrong very often on *The Bill* but when they did, it could be touch and go. A series of episodes featured PC Jim Carver turning into a helpless alcoholic. Mark Wingett was doing a terrific job and I felt honoured to be part of such a great storyline. In this one particular episode, we were shooting a scene in Kent which involved PC Jim Carver and Stamp escorting a van that is taking a load of confiscated drugs to be incinerated. My wicked sense of humour couldn't help wondering if the locals might get high as kites from the fumes. Anyway, we are behind a couple of police motor cyclists and start arguing about PC Jim Carver's drinking. All of a sudden he announces he is going to sick and asks me to stop the car. Stamp being Stamp replies, "You've got to be joking. You're not throwing up in here. You can be sick in your hat." But when Carver starts vomiting, Stamp is so disgusted, he pulls over.

By now the far from dynamic duo have lost sight of the convoy and when they do eventually catch up, it has been ambushed by robbers using a JCB. We set off in hot pursuit and I am having a right go at Carver while driving at top speed. But as we turn the corner, Sierra One comes under fire and the windscreen is shot out followed by the two front tyres.

To simulate the gunfire, the special effects team had placed small charges in the windscreen and the tyres. Using a remote control, these would go off in succession, as Sierra One rounded the corner. Well, once again, I was doomed when it came to special effects. Instead of going off one by one, all of the charges in the windscreen exploded at once. It was a real windscreen, rather than a fake made out of plastic and Mark and I were now covered in shards of glass. The team had no idea that something had gone wrong so then set off the charges in the tyres. By this time my hands were bleeding and my face was covered in tiny shards of glass, while Mark, who had been holding his knees up as Carver was still feeling sick, had pieces of glass embedded in both of them. I could hardly see where I was going but from my racing days I knew that the number one rule is never let go of the steering wheel so I held on for dear life.

When we stopped, the crew were shocked to see the state of us. Paramedics were on the scene pretty fast. Mark was in a lot of pain and his knees looked a mess. I was wearing my contact lenses but couldn't remove them myself in case glass had got into my eyes. We subsequently learnt that it had been decided that fitting a Perspex safety screen on the windscreen, was surplus to requirements and at £55 was too expensive. If I had known, I'd have paid the bloomin' money out of my own pocket.

One of the storylines I am most proud of is five-parter in 1998, when Stamp knocks over and kills a pedestrian. The tale kicks off with the episode Urgent Assistance. Always competitive, Stamp is wound up by Hollis' implication that PC Vicky Hagen (Samantha Robson) is a faster area car driver than him. As you can imagine, for Stamp, that is like a red rag to a bull. So when he gets a call from his beloved PC Polly Page for urgent assistance, accompanied by PC Dave Quinnan and youngster PC Luke Ashton (Scott Neal), he gets straight behind the wheel, with the blues and twos screeching at full volume. Already not thinking straight, when a short cut is blocked by a huge lorry, Stamp reverses at high speed back down the street. And despite a shouted warning from PC Dave Quinnan, he crashes straight into a young guy, Simon Attwell, who later dies in hospital.

It was an intricate stunt involving a stuntman and a ghostly looking dummy. But I am proud to say that I did all my own driving. I have only ever been stopped from carrying out two driving stunts. The first time was when a stuntman had to fly over the car bonnet. And the second was when Sierra One was involved in a crash and the team decided it was just too dangerous for an actor, no matter how much training and experience he had, to be put at risk.

And so begins probably the worst time of Stamp's life. He is suspended from driving until his trial for causing death by dangerous driving. And rumours spread like wildfire around Sun Hill, implying that he was racing PC Vicky Hagen (Samantha Robson) to the scene. Although shocked, Stamp firmly believes he did nothing wrong, lamenting, "I did everything right, I know I did." Yet there's still room for a spot of humour, even if it is a darker shade of black. "I went shopping yesterday," recalls Stamp, "I was that close to buying a Leonard Cohen album." Lovely line. The episode ends with Stamp confronting rumour monger PC Reg Hollis, who's been telling anyone who'll listen that Stamp was speeding. Pushing him up against the wall, he spits, "With your help they could put me way for 10 years." PC Hollis, always happy to state the obvious replies, "Tony, just because you're an advanced driver, doesn't mean you're superman."

But poor old Stamp never learns and in the second part, Taking Sides, he unwisely attends Simon's funeral. There he is confronted by his girlfriend who, unsurprisingly, is far from happy at seeing him. She accuses Stamp of harassment and removes the flowers Stamp has laid on the victim's grave. She then makes a formal complaint. Upset and irritable, Stamp goes back on duty and ends the day by arresting a chauffeur and ruining a bride's big day.

I, on the other hand, was having the time of my life. This was such a powerful story and a great challenge to me as an actor. I felt that I knew Stamp inside out, and yet there were still new areas to explore. He had always been so gung ho and yet now he was a timid shadow of his former self.

The next part, Deadly Impact, sees Stamp standing trial. Bad enough but while PC Ashton is witness for the defence, his best mate, PC Dave Quinnan is a witness for the prosecution. Understandably, this causes a rift in his friendship with Stamp. It is a huge relief when he is found not guilty of causing death by dangerous driving. However, he is found guilty of driving without due care and attention and fined £400. But there's no time for celebration when he is handed a summons outside the court, ordering him to appear before a police disciplinary board. One thing the audience and I learnt during the trial was that Stamp's middle name is John. PC Quinnan, also mentions that he is an expert in martial arts. Fortunately I already knew that. When an earlier episode required Stamp to teach a women's group the rudiments of self defence, being the king of research, I went to Hendon to work out with an instructor.

In the third instalment, Big Day, Stamp struggles with the hearing, despite being defended by James Bond's Miss Moneypenny, actress Samantha Bond (who is also the daughter of one of our former producers, the late Pat Sandys). Realising he could be facing the end of his police career, he walks out and is coaxed back by PC George Garfield (Huw Higginson). Filming the scene where he is found not guilty and reinstated, I was as over the moon as Stamp was. I too was not yet ready to leave the job I loved. We filmed these scenes at a genuine police head office and as I walked through the building, it was touching when quite a few coppers wished Stamp good luck.

Back on duty in Making Up, the viewers and I learnt more about Stamp. He had been in the job nearly 20 years; an area car driver for 11; had 10 accidents, one in a car park of all places, costing the force £16,000 in total. However, for both me and Stamp, the best moment of that episode has to be when he and PC Dave Quinnan make their peace.

I knew these episodes were good but it was the icing on the cake when I read the following review in *The Sun*:

*"The Bill's PC Tony Stamp has always been one of TV's best coppers. He might be as subtle as a stampeding police horse but he is just the sort of large and reliable officer you would want in an emergency. Until last night, that is, when his life fell apart on ITV after he knocked down and killed a pedestrian while rushing to save PC Polly Page from a violent drunk. Graham Cole's portrayal of the stunned Stamp was superb. His devastation at the death was quickly replaced by anger as be saw his proud career beginning to slip away from him. If the new hour-long editions of The Bill are all up to this standard, then there is plenty of life in it yet."*

Ironically I actually came close to knocking someone over once when shooting. There was always an element of danger when you were driving in real traffic. If I spotted a child or a dog I always stopped, much to the director's annoyance who accused me of breaking the flow of the scene. Surely better than running someone over? Yet ironically, the location of my near miss was when we were doing some technically difficult shots at Battersea Power Station in South London. What the director wanted was proving difficult. The first shot was to be of a man in a car on a spot of wasteland; next was Stamp and PC Dave Quinnan turning up in the police car; then close-ups of us and the villain. For some reason it just wasn't working. I had my foot on the accelerator for yet another shot, the crew and I were all ready to go when the director appeared at the last minute and gave me a few more notes. On set it is the first assistant director who shouts "Action!"' and "Cut!" So when I heard "Action!" I put my foot down. Unfortunately, at that precise moment the director darted in front of the car and disappeared. I was convinced I had hit him and he was now lying dead under the car. I got out and was relieved to find that he had managed to get out of the way. But I went ballistic at him, partly out of relief and partly because it was such a stupid thing to do, and as a director he should have known better.

Brenda Ennis, the producer had witnessed my 'tantrum' and I heard on the grapevine that she had commented, "Is that how he gets his performances?" I was furious that she or anyone else thought that was how I regularly behaved on set and so I went to see her the next day. "Do you have any idea how hard it is doing these car shots? I am driving while delivering four pages of dialogue. I can't hear the radio messages, as they are dubbed on afterwards, so have to imagine them in my head. I am sorry if I am sometimes a pain but it's only because I want to get it right." She was suitably apologetic.

Sometimes it was like being on a race track. The adrenalin was pumping. You listened carefully to the crews' radios as they attempted to hold back the traffic, "One line held, two held, what about three?" your foot would be hovering over the accelerator. Plus you also had to contend with wearing these stab vests, along with your uniform, which were really uncomfortable when in the car. The cameras were ready, you're trying to remember what to say and where to go and who on earth are you chasing and why. And then you'd hear, "Go, go go!" and you're off, into no man's land.

Obviously the units would do a recce of all the locations before we arrived to film. But a lot can happen in a few days. One time, they were planning to use part of the Croydon IKEA car park for a big car chase sequence, which involved Stamp. The store was still being built at the time. When we arrived on the Monday morning, a 20-foot wall had been demolished over the weekend, right in the middle of where the cars were scheduled to go. Another time, they wanted me to do a u-turn in the middle of a main road. I was a little concerned but they explained that when they did the recce, it was really quiet, so shouldn't be a problem. But when I arrived to film the scene, the road was busy. "When did you do the recce?" I asked. They replied last Saturday and couldn't understand why it was suddenly so busy. "Maybe," I volunteered, "It was quiet because it was the day of Princess

Diana's funeral."

On a lighter note there have been some truly bizarre events out on the streets. Once, I was sitting in Sierra One with Matthew Crompton, a nice lad who I shared my yoga tips with, who played PC Sam Harker, and later moved onto *Brookside* and *Coronation Street*. We were waiting to do the next scene when the radio crackled into life and we heard a police officer's voice. We knew that the police radios in our cars were on the same frequency as the real police so this cop had to be real. "Attention all units, if you see a young boy on a bike, detain him as the bike is stolen and he's just given me the one-finger salute."

Suddenly Matt and I spotted him, and I blurted into the radio, "He's just gone past us Sarge." "Well what are you waiting for, get him." Matt and I looked at each other and both agreed, we should do our duty, shouldn't we? And chased after him in the car. When we caught up with him, we could see he was confused. He recognised us and yet couldn't quite work out why. I slightly nudged the bike and he fell off. "You can't nick me, you're not even real coppers." "True," I replied, "but we have this thing called a citizen's arrest and you're nicked." It turned out that the stolen bike was a birthday present so the youngster was delighted to get it back the next day; and even better, it was presented by two coppers from *The Bill*.

The story even featured in *The Sun* newspaper:

*"A boy fleeing police on a stolen bicycle pedalled into a TV*

*shoot - and was nicked by telly cops from The Bill. Stars Graham Cole and Matthew Crompton - who play PCs Tony Stamp and Sam Harker - leapt from a patrol car to grab the lad, who first mistook them for real bobbies. The actors held the 14-year-old until genuine police arrived at an industrial estate in Mitcham, South London where scenes for the ITV cop show were being shot. A Bill insider said yesterday: 'The kid's eyes almost popped when he saw all the police uniforms on the film set.'"*

Unlike Andy, Jeff Stewart (PC Reg Hollis) was a great passenger. No matter how fast I went, he never said a thing. Whenever I asked him if he was okay, he would always say he was, "Absolutely fine."

I always loved filming in Central London and there was a funny incident when we were on location at Victoria Coach station. We had been given special permission to exceed the five miles per hour speed limit. So I drove Sierra One up at a mighty 20 miles per hour and then Clare Foster (PC Millie Brown) and I hopped out. In the story, Stamp and Brown are frantically searching for a young girl who is escaping on a coach but which one? As we started running in one direction, three young men suddenly started running in the other. They turned out to be a trio of illegal immigrants who mistook us for the real thing.

During all this time a member of the public had been standing watching proceedings. As I rushed past him for the umpteenth time, he asked, "You're Tony ain't it? *The Bill?*....You still in it?" I was in uniform at the time.

Another time we were filming outside a bank in Colliers Wood. There's a raid going on inside, and Stamp is waiting to nab the robbers when they try to make their getaway. I had spotted a chap sitting on a wall opposite. He had a briefcase, from which he produced a packed lunch and a flask. As I walked past, he looked at me and dryly said, "It's hardly Shakespeare is it?"

I am a stickler for research. For me it was never good enough just talking to the police advisers or reading the manual. That is why, ever since I joined *The Bill*, I worked closely with the real police. And I think it paid off. I was enormously proud when, on my *This is Your Life*, I heard presenter Michael Aspel say that, "According to the real police, Stamp is the most convincing copper on the box." High praise indeed and I think partly due to my meticulous research.

When you first arrive on the show, you are encouraged to go out with the police a few times, to get a feel of what it's really all about. Some of the cast have been reluctant but I liked it so much that I continued and have built up a great array of contacts and friends in the force, along with some priceless tips. I listen carefully to what they say and hope I put what I have learnt to good use; making my performance as PC Stamp, as real as possible. Some of my colleagues questioned why I bothered and reminded me that I was not a real copper. I just gave them a withering stare and replied, "Yeah, but I'm still here." And of course I managed to out-stay nearly all of them.

My research was invaluable when I was shooting the five-parter. I asked Trevor Hermes, one of the police advisers, if he could put me in touch with any police officers who had been in a similar situation to Stamp. He came up with about four, two of whom proved perfect. There was one guy who had knocked a kid off his bike; thankfully he didn't kill him. But for several weeks afterwards, he would sleep outside his own children's bedrooms as a form of penance. Hearing that really helped me to further understand what Stamp was going through and convey his inner pain.

And I have witnessed some sad sights, involving domestic violence. The police turn up at the door and a three-year-old opens it. Mum is covered in blood and dad is swilling back lager, watching the telly as if nothing has happened.

One of the scariest incidents I have ever experienced, when out with the police, happened in South London. I was out with a squad in a patrol car in the early hours when a car rushed past with no lights on. Apparently this is standard behaviour if a car has been nicked. Having spotted the police, the driver did a u-turn and we followed it into a side street. As the cops were checking whether it had been stolen, the driver suddenly put his hand on the horn, and kept it there, waking up the entire street. Lights started going on and people came out on the street. When they saw the patrol car, the mood changed and they started shouting abuse. By now I was scared. This wasn't the time to be heroic, so we cut our losses and reversed out of the street like a bat out of hell.

Thanks to my work in the health service, I still have a strong stomach. So when I was invited to accompany the police to an unexplained death, I did not hesitate. The coppers had to kick the door in and what they found was the body of an pensioner. The poor soul had been lying there for some time so the smell was horrendous. The entire flat was infested by maggots and flies. As we waited for the coroner to arrive, I had a look around. One of the saddest things was his phone bill. It was a meagre £22, which covered the rental. Tragically, it appeared that no one was going to miss the deceased.

But it wasn't all doom and gloom. One time when I was out with some real police who were members of the Flying Squad at a charity do they bet me £100 to wear one of their ties in a *Bill* scene. Now Stamp is predominantly in uniform and a mauve tie with an eagle was hardly discreet. It took me nigh on 10 months but when Stamp is standing in the dock accused of running over that pedestrian, I am wearing that tie. I got the cheque with a note saying, "You swine." And I gave it to charity.

During another day out with the cops, we were called to a posh address after reports of two well dressed men fighting in the street. The officers couldn't understand why they recognised the address until they turned up to discover the duty solicitor fighting with his neighbour over a wheelie bin.

One of the funniest incidents was when we arrived at a punch up at a Pizza Hut in South London. Obviously I am in civvies when I shadow the police but when we walked in, the lads immediately recognised me. They stopped fighting and jeered, "I know you, you ain't no real police, you're all actors," and resumed fighting again. They were very surprised when the handcuffs appeared.

I've also been out on a few drugs raids. One was particularly memorable. I attended the briefing at four in the morning and then travelled to a known crack house, which the drugs squad had been watching for weeks. After a couple of hours hiding outside, the guys were getting ready to strike when I felt this tap, tap on my shoulder. I turned around and there was a fan, brandishing a piece of paper and holding a pen, "Can I have your autograph please?" I pulled her down and explained that she needed to be quiet as we were filming. She got her autograph. Back at the station, one of the most notorious drugs barons who had been arrested called me over and shook my hand. "Man, you're a legend." Unreal.

Not every night is full of incident and on one such occasion there wasn't much happening so the lads suggested livening things up by heading over to 'Cynthia Payne country' to see what was going on. Cynthia Payne was a notorious brothel keeper who kept an orderly house in Streatham, South London. She was infamous for using a system of payment involving luncheon vouchers. Watching clients coming and going was fascinating. On the way back the cops pulled over a couple of known prostitutes. As I stood there watching, one of them suddenly shouted, "Oi, you, get your hands off my tits!" I was mortified but the officers burst out laughing. "Don't worry, she's always doing that."

I like to give something back and remain heavily involved in a range of police charities and go to as many functions as I can. When I was in *The Bill*, I regularly attended police open days, often turning up in Sierra One, and happily posed for pictures with the car. I suppose you could liken my relationship over the years with Sierra One to that of Michael Knight (David Hasselhoff) and

KITT in *Knight Rider*. Though, of course, Sierra One couldn't talk.

I was enormously proud when a group of young officers told me that they had been inspired to join the police by PC Stamp. He was exactly the kind of policeman they wanted to be.

Playing Stamp introduced me to so many people I would probably otherwise never have met. Once I attended an awards ceremony where fellow guests included Sir Ian Blair, who was the Metropolitan Police Commissioner at the time, the now former Home Secretary Jackie Smith and HRH Prince Charles. As always I couldn't resist being a bit cheeky and said, "Sir Ian, you are my sixth Commissioner; Miss Smith I have lost count of the number of Home Secretaries I have served under. And Your Royal Highness, I trust I will still be walking the streets of Sun Hill on your Coronation." I think they liked it. Okay, it never happened, but it was still a good joke at the time.

Being on *The Bill* has certainly opened some doors that otherwise would have been locked. For example, I was lucky enough to get to go up in India 99, the Metropolitan Police's helicopter. I remember being at Scotland Yard once and a commander told me. "I've tried to go on it and they wouldn't take me!" And one of *The Bill*'s police advisors Trevor Hermes, a former inspector who had been a copper for 22 years once said to me, "You've met more commanders and commissioners than I have!"

And I once met Detective Chief Superintendent Jack Slipper, who was known as Slipper of the Yard. He was in charge of the investigation into the Great Train Robbery, back in 1963. When I asked him why he had kept chasing the likes of Ronnie Biggs, he replied, "Because I knew they did it."

Because of my work with the police, I was sometimes critical of storylines. When PC Nick Klein (Rene Zagger) was having drug problems, I argued that as police officers we were trained to notice drug abuse so he wouldn't have been able to hide his problem for long. I think they heeded my words because I only ever had one episode with former *EastEnder* Todd Carty, who played PC Gabriel Kent, who turned out to be a nasty piece of work, going on to shoot two coppers and rape three. I had really enjoyed working with Todd and wondered why there were no plans for us to work together more. I was told it was because Stamp would suss him out in no time.

The police have always been enormously welcoming towards *The Bill* and never more so when a group of us travelled to Dublin for Huw Higginson's (PC George Garfield) stag night. During our momentous pub crawl, we were invited in to practically every police station in the city, where a few pints of Guinness were waiting. The next morning I was playing in a charity golf match and was so hungover that I had to pay a young lad to put the ball on the tee. If I had tried, I would probably have fallen head first onto the bunker.

But sometimes *The Bill* got it wrong. Amusingly, the police were far from impressed when PC Reg Hollis became the Police Federation rep on screen. They weren't keen on a bumbling cop representing their union. But he was very diligent. And when a couple of CID Officers visited the set, they were horrified to see desks covered in file cases, explaining the contents were confidential and shouldn't be left lying around, where anyone could take a peek. The desks look a lot tidier now.

I have met plenty of coppers who are older than me and still in the service. In fact there is a trend now towards hanging on to older cops by forming task forces, like in that wonderful TV show, *New Tricks*, starring Dennis Waterman and James Bolam. So I always thought there was plenty of life left in Stamp yet. And I was affectionately known as Daddy Cole, so maybe Stamp could have been Sun Hill's wise and trusted father figure. But as we now know that was not meant to be.

# CHAPTER NINE

# Pardon?

I have always prided myself on being in good health and feel blessed to have rarely been ill in my life. While working in the health service, I learnt the importance of looking after oneself. And as a regular in a successful TV show you are a slave to an incredibly tight shooting schedule, so unless you are dying, the show must go on. You simply cannot afford to be ill. Once while I was in *The Bill*, I was in agony with toothache but I still had to wait 13 weeks before I could make an appointment to see a dentist due to filming commitments.

I try to keep fit. I have one of those ski machines that won't injure your back, as I still have the odd twinge following that fall I had in custody. I tried jogging but was always being recognised. I got so fed up that I hung up my running shoes. The women would shout, "Nice legs!" which I suppose is a compliment. While the men, thinking they were being witty, would call after me, "He went that way!" Being spotted with a big red face wasn't something I relished. And camera phones only made it worse. I had visions of ending up on the pages of one of the tabloids with some dreadful headline, highlighting how out of shape I was.

We briefly had a gym at *The Bill* but it was disbanded in case the actors did themselves an injury. Which inevitably someone would!

I'm careful about my diet but I am definitely someone who lives to eat so I have to be diligent. Cherry is a vegetarian but that's not for me. The problem when you are filming is there is always a mountain of food available. And like Worzel Gummidge, I am rather partial to an afternoon cup of tea accompanied by a slice of cake. I used to use PC Stamp as an excuse, saying that a thin Stamp wouldn't be right. After all he is a bachelor so he probably lives on takeaways, especially curries. Obviously I can't use that line anymore so I have to be more careful than ever about what I eat.

During my early days as Stamp, I was often chasing villains on foot, jumping over walls and fences. Sometimes I got injured and had to be taken to hospital for stitches and sprains. But never anything major. So when I was diagnosed with a debilitating health problem it was one hell of a shock.

It started in 1992, when I began to experience strange noises in my ears. The first time it happened was after I had played a game of squash. Nothing unusual about that as I tried to play at least once a week. But as I was bending down in the changing room, tying up my laces, I heard what I can only describe as a banging noise in my ears. It was a bit like someone blowing in your ear. And that was all I could hear, any other sounds were suddenly muted. It reminded me of the sensation you have when your ears are full of water after swimming. Being an old trouper,

I didn't think too much about it. And I really couldn't spend time indulging in an ailment that didn't appear to be anything important, just annoying. Anyway, over time, as the frequency increased, I got used to the 'whooshing' sound in my ears.

But Cherry was worried in case it was high blood pressure or cholesterol and suggested I went to see my GP, which, after a lot of well meaning nagging, eventually I did. I can remember the day as if it were yesterday. He started peering in my ears, using an instrument I now know is called an Otoscope. Being nervous, the whooshing, which would increase when I was stressed, was louder than ever. After a good look around, the doctor passed judgement. "Graham, you have the early signs of tinnitus." Although I was relieved to have some sort of diagnosis, I had never heard of tinnitus. "Pardon?"

He went on to explain that tinnitus can affect one or both ears and patients usually describe it as a ringing noise, but in some cases it can take the form of a high pitched whining noise, buzzing, hissing, screaming, humming, whistling, or, in my case, a 'whooshing' sound. Being a straight talking kind of guy, I cut straight to the chase. "Are you trying to tell me I am going deaf?" He wasn't sure and being a GP and not a specialist, didn't like to commit. But one thing he did know; there was nothing he could do so I resigned myself to having to live with it. I wasn't happy but what could I do? He was the doctor. And despite my past experience in the health service, I was reluctant to probe any further. A case of burying my head in the sand and getting on with it.

I've always been interested in 'mind over matter' and I do yoga, so I began using that to calm myself down at bedtime. I almost hypnotised myself into trying to ignore the sounds in my ears so that I could fall asleep. But during the day, running after villains on the streets of Sun Hill only made the whooshing worse. And over the next few months, the whooshing got louder and louder. I held out for as long as I could but after 18 months I was at the end of my tether so I went back to my GP. He referred me to see an ear, nose and throat specialist which, looking back, he probably should have done in the first place.

I was quite looking forward to my complaint being analysed by an expert but I was to be both disappointed and alarmed. Barely drawing breath for an introduction, the specialist launched immediately into a hearing test. As I strained to hear the differing sounds, he kept his head firmly down so I had no idea how I was doing. After what seemed an eternity, he finally looked up and said that I had Otosclerosis, which sounded to me like the name of some long forgotten pop star but is actually a hardening of the stirrup bone in the middle ear. As I tried to get my head around this, he bluntly announced that the prognosis was bad. The tests had shown that I had already lost some of my hearing and the noise in my ears was only going to get progressively worse. Then he casually delivered the killer blow. "You're going deaf," and that was it. No "I'm sorry" or "but we can do something about it." Nothing. Not even an idea about when I might go deaf. Tomorrow perhaps or in 10 years time? For once I was speechless. Heartbreaking thoughts began racing through my head. Did this mean that I would never again hear birdsong in the morning? Or hear my children tell me what they had been up to at school that day? Or my daughter Laura say "I do" on her wedding day?

I was shell-shocked. I didn't know what to say or do. But there was one thing I was certain of. Whatever the prognosis, there was no way I wanted to be treated by this particular doctor, whatever he offered. His people skills left a lot to be desired. Having worked in the health service, I knew it shouldn't be this clinical. In a monotone voice, he continued by explaining that the otosclerosis had caused a form of tinnitus called pulsatile tinnitus, which typically affects women more than men. It tends to synchronise itself with the heart beat. So what I was really hearing was the beating of my own heart. A disturbing thought. There was nothing wrong with the actual ear and its hearing ability; it was the mechanism that was faulty.

When he mentioned wearing a hearing aid I agreed, especially as it meant it could be fitted by a technician rather than him. Not only would it help me hear but would also partially blot out the tinnitus noise. The technician was a kind soul and told me that the hearing loss would not happen overnight, it would be gradual. She mentioned there was a surgical procedure to correct otosclerosis but, and here was another dose of bad news, there was a one in 400 risk of permanent deafness immediately after surgery. Or the hearing loss can return again further down the years. I decided to give it a miss and try the hearing aid first.

Luckily hearing aids are a lot less visible than they were but I knew I couldn't wear one when I was filming. And anyway, in the end it proved more bother than it was worth as it often made a high pitched whistling noise which was worse than the constant whooshing noise.

So I resolved to get the better of my deafness by teaching myself to lip read. This worked as long as people were facing towards me. But at showbiz parties or meetings, involving groups of people, I struggled as I couldn't always see them. And when I did get involved in a conversation I found it really hard to focus as I couldn't separate the different sounds. I told everyone, including the bosses at *The Bill*, who were very understanding. I needed my colleagues to know that when I didn't answer, I wasn't being rude, I just couldn't hear them. Of course whenever I mentioned I was hard of hearing, nearly everyone asked, "Pardon?" It didn't take long for this to become extremely irritating. Especially when it became a running joke on set. But, as always, I smiled sweetly and got on with the job.

I joined a tinnitus help group which really helped. Meeting others who were all in the same boat proved a real release. Only they could truly understand what it was like to live with the fact that you were going deaf. Some members were trying to keep their condition a secret from their families but I thought they must have an idea. And anyway, surely it was better that they knew so that they understood why sometimes your behaviour was a bit odd.

I know I was driving my own family mad. I thought I was dealing with the situation pretty well but I wasn't. For example, I didn't realise that when I was talking, I was whispering. Or that the TV or sound system was so loud it was reverberating throughout the whole house. Instead of Cherry telling the kids to turn down their music, she had to bellow at me. Neither could I hear the racket the kids were making in the back of the car. But Cherry could. And it was Cherry who had to constantly point these incidents out to me. And the whooshing was getting louder. It was the first sound I heard in the morning and the last one I heard at night. Sleep was an escape. I have since found a book on living with tinnitus called *When Silence is a Stranger* written by David Shepherd. It depicts exactly how a sufferer never has a moment's peace from the noise in their ears. And how the condition can slowly drive you insane.

I was coping, just about, on the set of *The Bill* thanks to the lip reading. But scenes where I had to enter a room after someone had spoken were hard as I couldn't hear them and, being the other side of the door, couldn't see them to lip read. I had to get a member of the crew, on my side of the door, to give me my cue. By now I had lost a third of my hearing.

In 2000 things finally came to a head during a night shoot with *The Bill*. The storyline involved a child being kidnapped and we were on location in some fields. I was already worried as I knew it would be dark and the actors would be spread out so I wouldn't be able to see their faces. A further concern was that all the actors in the scene were guest artistes so they didn't know I was hard of hearing. And I felt uncomfortable asking them to make allowances. So, to be on the safe side, I learnt the entire script. It was a freezing cold winter's night so fortunately I could see the hot breath coming off the actors when they spoke and when that disappeared, I was able to work out it was my turn to speak. But I was so stressed that I might miss my cue that the whooshing sound in my ears became almost unbearable. It was at that moment, in a field in the middle of nowhere, that I realised I couldn't go on like this. So when I got home the following morning, I told Cherry I had to have that operation. She was concerned but knew how hard it was becoming for me and gave her full support.

I was nervous but I thought anything is better than this. I was lucky enough to be referred to top surgeon David Golding-Wood. He was a pioneer of not only this type of surgery, but also operating on foetuses within the womb. I warmed to him immediately, especially when he asked Cherry how my tinnitus was affecting her. After all, she was having to live with it too. I also liked his honesty. He drew a diagram to illustrate the problem and went through the details of the operation, step by step. And he explained the dangers; there was a high risk of complete deafness as a result of shock waves going through the inner ear during surgery or from infection or changes in ear pressure. But I had come this far and couldn't go back now. If there was even the remotest chance of stopping that never-ending whooshing noise, I had to take it.

Mr Golding-Wood would only operate on one ear, in case anything went wrong. That way, at least I had a remnant of hearing left in the other ear. The right one was the worst so that was the one he operated on under general anesthetic.

In a procedure called a stapedotomy, Mr Golding-Wood

removed the stapes, the stirrup based small bones in the ear, and replaced them with an artificial 'bone.' This prosthesis, or plastic replacement, is shaped like a question mark and needs to fit precisely. If it was too loose, the hearing would be impaired and if too tight, it would disturb the blood flow to the bone.

The operation took four hours and Cherry tells me they were the longest four hours of her life. Thankfully the operation was a complete success and I cannot describe the feeling of being able to hear again. As I came round from the anesthetic, I could not believe that I could hear the nurses' knees rubbing together and their skirts rustling. Everything was so loud but gloriously so. Mr Golding-Wood told me that this was a normal sensation and once my brain adjusted, that acute level of hearing would become normal. After the op, my ear was packed with dressings and I was told to avoid violent movements, coughing and sneezing over the next few days.

As Cherry drove me home, I had to ask her to slow down as I could hear the tyres turning. Excuse the pun, but the sound was deafening. It was the most extraordinary sensation and as the surgeon had predicted, the level of hearing gradually returned to normal. When, a few days later they took the dressings off and the whole world came flooding in.

I still have tinnitus in my left ear but I can cope with that as the level of whooshing is greatly reduced. I actually think the hearing in my right ear is better than Cherry's. I still cannot decide whether to have my left ear done. Apparently a second surgical procedure for otosclerosis has a whole new set of risks, including damage to the nerve which supplies taste to the tongue. And I do like my food.

I have been warned that my newly acquired hearing may not last for life but I am thrilled with the new lease of life it's given me.

Nobody seems quite sure what actually causes tinnitus. Being a nosey parker, I've done extensive research of my own and consulted my old and battered copy of Grey's Anatomy from my days as a porter. Tinnitus is not a disease but a symptom of a variety of causes including anything from ear infections or wax; foreign objects in the ear, nose allergies or injury from loud noises. When I was on stage there were plenty of loud bangs, especially in pantomime. And I do wonder if some damage was done to my nose during my rugby playing days. According to the Royal National Institute for the Deaf, tinnitus affects 4.7 million people in the UK. Some estimate that as many as one in three people over 65 have some degree of tinnitus. And probably don't even know it.

There are a host of famous sufferers too, including Michelangelo, Ludwig Van Beethoven, Barbra Streisand and Eric Clapton. But then again, there's an infamous few, including Adolf Hitler and Gary Glitter.

Other than being deaf, I have only ever had one other tricky health scare. One Christmas Cherry bought me a bike and like a kid with a new toy, I couldn't wait to play with it. It had been a tough couple of weeks at *The Bill* before the break. I had been shuffling between five units. Schedules were tighter than ever, as the show took a two-week break over Christmas and tempers were fraught. To cope I had been adding the odd dash of scotch to my coffee. I don't drink a lot but I needed something to keep me going. So on Boxing Day Cherry, Matthew, Laura and I went for a bike ride in some woodland near our house. We were almost at the top of a hill when I fell off and, in Cherry's words, "was unconscious and turning blue." She was convinced I was having a heart attack. The kids started crying but just as Cherry was about to call for an ambulance, I regained consciousness. I insisted I was fine but Cherry was having none of it and when we got home, she shoved me in the car and drove me to A & E at our local hospital.

On arrival I was immediately given an ECG test to check my heart. The doctor was concerned by the results which revealed a rapid heartbeat and decided the only way to slow it down was to stop the heart and start it again. Now I didn't like the sound of that. And nor did poor Matthew who subsequently fainted and hit his head on a trolley. So poor Cherry now had not one patient but two to worry about. As Matthew was being treated for concussion, I suggested that if the doctor left me in the cubicle for about 20 minutes, I would be able to slow my heart down myself. He was understandably sceptical but left just the same. As you now know, I am very interested in the power of the mind and am able to calm myself down using self hypnosis. Regularly combining yoga with self hypnosis has helped me stay calm and even cured a problem I was having with recurrent migraines. So when the doctor returned and checked my pulse, he was astonished to find my heartbeat was back to normal. He agreed to discharge me as long as I saw a heart specialist.

So, for peace of mind, I went to see a specialist for an examination. I was convinced I was okay but felt it better to be safe than sorry. It was all very thorough. Firstly my blood pressure was taken and found to be a little too high but I'm sure that's because I was anxious about being tested. And different staff kept coming in and out of the room every few seconds, which was very off-putting.

Next, I had to run on a treadmill which was not very pleasant. Especially as they had a crash team behind me, just in case I had a heart attack. I was then strapped to a bed that whizzed around at high velocity, a bit like a poor man's aerodynamic test. Apparently most people pass out but I was fine. Maybe all that whizzing around in Sierra One had prepared me.

Finally I was given a local anesthetic so that a tiny camera could be inserted into my leg to have a good look around. Now as you know I am not squeamish but there is something slightly odd about watching a screen that is showing your own insides. There was my heart, pumping away. And every so often it would jump thanks to a series of electric charges testing its reactions. But it kept on pumping. This particular doctor was a huge fan of *The Bill* and as I watched the screen, all I could hear was him saying, in his Australian twang, "Wait until I tell my mum back home that I was examining PC Tony Stamp." Excitedly, he then dragged in a colleague, who was in the middle of carrying out a heart bypass next door, and covered in blood, which was a bit disconcerting, to meet me.

By now the room was getting a little overcrowded as a group of medical students had piled in to watch the main attraction, 'The Heart-Stopping Graham Cole Show.' Bad enough but when he announced, "Now here is something we don't see ..." my heart sank, metaphorically of course. Was there really something wrong with me? Was my heart packing up? He continued, "...as often as we would like. This is a healthy heart telling us to clear off and leave it alone." Relief swept over me. Normal service was promptly resumed when a student asked for my autograph.

The Aussie explained that he thought my episode had been caused by the scotch. He had seen an RAF pilot the previous week. "A similar thing happened to him; he hadn't been drinking but he had a panic attack, causing his heart to start beating faster and he lost consciousness. But this happened at 47,000 feet in the air. Luckily the auto pilot kicked in." I couldn't help thinking that particular situation wasn't similar to mine at all but I didn't like to argue.

He elaborated, explaining how a job such as those of a footballer, pilot, and doctor or, in my case an actor, was particularly stressful. "For you Mr Cole, every day is like sitting an exam. You learn your lines the night before and have to get it right the next day. The adrenalin kicks in and the heart beats faster to help the body keep on top of the situation. But sometimes it's a little too much. Especially if alcohol is involved." He pronounced me fit and well but advised laying off the scotch for a while, which I did.

His words came back to me a few months later when I was on set with Lisa Geoghan (PC Polly Page) doing a scene in St Hugh's. The director, who I think thought he was making a documentary, not a television drama in deepest Merton, was keen on realism so insisted that Lisa be attached to the heart monitor. Her heart was pumping normally. Hardly surprising as here she was in a situation she was comfortable with, filming a routine scene. But when the guest artiste was hooked up, he was so nervous, his heart was going ballistic and they had to switch the monitor off.

Personally I thought the whole exercise was trite and unkind for the guest artiste. And if my memory serves me right, in the end they didn't even use the scene.

# CHAPTER TEN

# Ding Dong

I have always loved appearing on other TV shows so when *The Bill* was invited on to *Noel's House Party,* I jumped at the chance. Back in the 1990s the BBC1 show, presented by Noel Edmonds, was the biggest thing on television. Broadcast live, which I love, on Saturday nights, it was a ratings winner. Everybody wanted to join in the fun down at the fictitious Crinkley Bottom and be squashed by a pink blob called Mr Blobby. Of the cast, only Andy Paul (PC Dave Quinnan) and I accepted the invitation. So, unsure of what to do, we decided to sing.

Our duet was well received and we both had a great time. Afterwards, in the green room, where the guests hang out, I got chatting to one of the writers, Charlie Adams. Not shy of coming forward, I made it clear that both of us would love to come back and were pretty much up for anything. Neither of us thought that much about it so I was genuinely surprised when Charlie phoned me at home a few days later. "I've had this idea about a sketch involving two CID officers. Would *The Bill* allow you to do something like that?" "Of course," I replied, "I'll run it past the executive producer."

But my bravado was an act. Michael Chapman was the executive producer at the time and was a formidable character. A former Royal Navy officer, and producer of such seventies TV classics as *Public Eye* and *Enemy at the Door*, he was very much of the old school and despite working in television, he never watched it. He wasn't very keen on publicity either and never understood the benefits of appearing on other people's shows. So we knew we had a battle on our hands.

Both Andy and I were nervous wrecks when we went to see Michael in his office, located in an area of *The Bill* base known as the flight deck. He was every inch the Captain and people used to say that his bark was worse than his bite but I can't say there was much in it.

Being the louder of the two, I did the talking. My palms were sweating and, as I began to speak, I could detect a slight crack in my voice. "Mr Chapman, Andy and I appeared on *Noel's House Party* last week and it went very well. I don't know if you saw it?" He shook his head. Not a good start. I continued, "They've invited us back and suggested we play a couple of CID officers so that it's clear we are not playing the same roles as we do in *The Bill*." I then went on to explain how beneficial our appearance would be to *The Bill*. "We are two of the stars of one of ITV's biggest shows and we'll be appearing on the BBC's flagship show, seen by millions on a Saturday night. Despite not being in uniform, the audience know us from *The Bill* and Noel will introduce us as the boys from *The Bill*. So it will be fantastic PR for the show."

Michael, who was a man of few words, listened intently. He

asked me to describe the show a little more and winced when I mentioned the gunge tank. After what seemed like ages, the man from *The Bill* said yes. I knew he had a mischievous side and I think the idea of two ITV stars on a top BBC show appealed to him. Andy and I were beside ourselves. Little did we know that for the next few years, we would have to go through this charade every single time we were invited onto the show which, in the end, was practically every week.

But Michael, who ruled *The Bill* with a rod of iron, was rarely that easy to turn. When a director approached me about appearing in a TV drama set during the Falklands War, I was really interested. The part was based on a Lieutenant who was horrified by the army's lack of preparation and equipment. They didn't even have anyone who could speak Spanish so they could communicate, when necessary, with the Argentineans. So, in spite of being awarded medals, when he returned home, he refused to shake Margaret Thatcher's hand.

It was a great role but Michael would not give way. "It's a uniformed character and it will only confuse the audience," and that was that.

I was allowed to do a film for the British Film Council called *Millennium Madness* in the late nineties. Everyone was obsessed with the millennium as it drew closer so when stunt co-ordinator Stuart St Paul asked me if I would appear in his children's film about an imagined aftermath of the millennium, I didn't think twice. It was filmed in just five days during the Christmas break and was absolutely freezing. It was set around Christmas Eve and

I played the dad, reading a post apocalyptic story to my children. But when the story came alive, I was also the villain – Mustdad - trying to capture a group of children. Sadly, despite poor Stuart re-mortgaging his house, the production values weren't as good as they should have been. And even with a special screening in Hollywood plus a DVD release, the film never really took off. But I had a great time and I do love playing villains; far more fun.

Like every actor on the planet I have always dreamt of being a Hollywood star. But over the years I've witnessed many an actor leave *The Bill* and head for Hollywood, never to be heard of again. So I know the reality. Very few American actors make it, never mind us Brits. At least being in *The Bill* meant I was something of a household name and from time to time I have had a faint glimmer of what it must be like to be on the Hollywood A List. But I did have a brief taste of life in Tinsel Town when *Millennium Madness* was shown at a film festival in Hollywood. During my whistle stop tour I was invited to a party in Beverley Hills at the home of Steven E de Souza, the writer of the hugely successful *Die Hard* movies, which starred Bruce Willis.

It really was a case of how the other half live. It was a Halloween party, a festival Americans take very seriously indeed so no guessing what the theme was – ghost and ghouls - though luckily I wasn't expected to be attired as either. We were all picked up in black hearses and taken to a magnificent mansion located far up in the Hills, the higher you are, the wealthier you must be. It had a sweeping drive and was surrounded by beautifully manicured lawns. I could barely contain my excitement although

I was a little disappointed that Bruce himself wasn't one of the guests!

There were 'bodies' in the pool – they were actually dummies and a plastic hand was submerged slightly below the service, just like the one in the final scene of the film *Carrie* that grabs actress Amy Irving as she places flowers outside Carrie's dilapidated house. Every few minutes this plastic hand would do just that, seemingly appearing from nowhere and grabbing an arm or a leg, giving unsuspecting guests a real fright. There was an enormous Pavlova in the shape of a mummy and the waiters were all dressed as Dracula. Most of them out of work actors, still chasing their dream and giving me a wakeup call before I got too carried away, thinking maybe I should give it a go. Okay, I never will be a Hollywood star but I haven't done too badly. And I can dream can't I? But it was an amazing experience that I wouldn't have missed for the world

When Andy Paul and I were doing *Noel's House Party,* we would get to the BBC Studios in Shepherds Bush, West London at about 3pm on a Saturday afternoon. We had been sent a script but being live television, there were always last minute changes. We would rehearse with Noel and then Andy would disappear to the next door studio that housed the sports show *Grandstand.* As a football nut, he was in seventh heaven, watching one of the games and seeing the results come in. I on the other hand, would have a kip in our dressing room.

About an hour before the show began, we would go into makeup and then add the finishing touch, those rather fetching beige macs. We'd be called to the back of the stage approximately 10 minutes before our bit. We never knew how long we would have to wait as being a live show, anything could happen. In semi darkness, Andy and I would climb up some flimsy stairs and onto an eight feet by 10 feet plinth. As we listened to Noel and the audience, the adrenalin started pumping. Being before the op, my ears would start whooshing but nothing could take away from the magic of that moment, waiting to go on. Andy and I had both learnt our lines but they were displayed on an autocue just in case. But being a stubborn old pro, I never looked at it.

All of a sudden the lights would go up, the bell would ring, ding dong and Noel would open the door; the audience would start cheering wildly when they saw us. As the noise subsided, Andy would begin informing Noel what the Crinkley police had been up to that week. There were plenty of corny lines. One of my favourites was when Andy reported that we had just come hot foot from a stake out. Dry as a bone, I would add, "I had chips with mine." In no time that became our catchphrase and despite the audience knowing it was coming, the line worked every time.

We got on very well with Noel, who especially liked our professionalism and we were delighted to become a regular item on the show. By now other cast members were sniffing around but it was too late, Andy and I were established as a permanent fixture on one of the most popular shows on British TV.

Noel, Andy and I were always getting the giggles and all three of us would dissolve into helpless laughter many a time. One of the most memorable sketches featured a Scottish pickpocket called Hamish McFlynn. The joke was that he was so sleight of hand that he could have your braces away before you knew it. Right on cue, my trousers would promptly fall down.

The BBC wardrobe department suggested I have a practice. So Cherry and I spent hours trying to work out how to make the trousers fall down on cue. But nothing worked. At the studio, even with the help of wardrobe, none of us could get the gag to work.

So in the end, I was standing on the plinth, waiting for the door to open with my hands in the pockets of the mac literally holding the trousers up, with my backside hanging out. Not a pretty sight. The trousers didn't have to fall until near the end of the sketch, and by then I was hanging on for dear life. When I eventually let go, it got a great laugh but do you think I could pull them back up? Noel and Andy were creased up, and as the door was still open, so was the audience. Once, when asked why *Noel's House Party* was so successful, Noel replied that it was because it was live and viewers responded to that, as it added an element of both surprise and danger. He was so right.

I loved working with Andy anyway and we had a great time on Noel's show. We also did a few pantomimes together. One year Andy was playing Jack in *Jack and the Beanstalk* and I was Fleshcreep, the giant's 'little' helper. *The Bill* schedule was so full on that we only had four days of rehearsal, which was pretty scary. Being a bit of a panto old hand myself, I re-did all the lighting and the sound to bring it up to date.

For the big climax of the show, Andy and I had a terrific sword fight to do. Both of us put everything we had ever seen on the big screen into it. I think we were both modelling ourselves on Errol Flynn in *Robin Hood*. There was a great moment when I would get hold of Jack and ask the kids whether I should kill him? Kids being kids all shouted "Kill him!" so I stepped forward and said, "I think you've missed the concept of all this." The parents were literally rolling in the aisles.

Much as I loved working with Andy we did have a slight falling out during the run. Being an old hand at theatre I assumed Andy knew about the tradition of first night presents. The stars usually give out pressies, only little trinkets, even daft ones, to all the cast and crew on opening night as a thank you, and hoping they "break a leg." When he spotted me distributing mine he was livid, saying I should have told him. But all was well in the end when he sent out for drinks for the after show party. However, I'm not sure if he ever believed it was a genuine mistake on my part. Well Andy I assure you it was.

The panto was a huge success and we were asked if we fancied doing Sadler's Wells next year. Unfortunately it never happened. The rule was that you could do panto as long as you were close to *The Bill* base, in case you were needed in a hurry. Kevin Lloyd, being Kevin, took no notice and went off to Birmingham without telling anyone. Michael Chapman was furious and banned any of us from doing panto from then on, a rule still in place at *The Bill* to this day. The producers argue that it's too disruptive to production. I miss it terribly as I really love doing it but rules are rules. Now I've left *The Bill* though, hopefully there's nothing to stop me returning to the boards; every cloud has a silver lining. However, one cast member, who remains nameless, broke the rules a few years ago and had to pay his entire panto fee to *The Bill*.

Cherry, Matthew and Laura used to accompany me to the *Noel's House Party* studio. The kids especially loved meeting the bands especially Boyzone or another teenage sensation at the time, Hanson. Anyone that was anyone appeared on Noel's show, including the late *EastEnders* star Wendy Richard, Leslie Grantham and even Edwina Currie got gunged. It happened just once to me and that was quite enough. I myself was star struck by Sir Roger Moore who was a real gentleman. Whenever I met him at charity gigs, he said how much he'd like to appear in an episode of *The Bill*. Sadly it never happened during my time on the show. I wasn't particularly impressed by David Hasselhoff. He had a huge entourage with him and also seemed much too reliant on his autocue.

*Noel's House Party* was so successful that Noel opened a theme park called Crinkley Bottom in Morecambe in 1994 and Andy and I were there for the opening. I thought it was going to be a sure fire winner but sadly it closed after only 13 weeks which just shows how you never can tell what's going to take off with the good British public. More successful was when Noel took the house party on the road, visiting holiday camps including Butlins and Pontins, during the summer season. Andy was unable to appear but I was delighted to reprise one half of the comedy duo. Tony Blackburn was part of the show. And before he was really famous, *Men Behaving Badly* star Neil Morrissey had a small part as the window cleaner.

Noel knew how much I loved driving and that I was in possession of a full racing licence. So when he invited me to a festival at Castle Combe racetrack in Wiltshire, I was devastated to have to turn it down due to filming commitments. The event was on a Sunday but *The Bill* was behind schedule so I had been called in. We were filming in Hendon until lunchtime so there was no way I could get there. But Noel had other ideas. "I'll send my helicopter and you can bring Cherry and the kids too." We were filming an episode featuring PC Mike Jarvis, Stephen Beckett, (who went on to *Coronation Street* as Josh Peacock's real dad) attending a driving course and Stamp was showing him how to do it. So at precisely 12.30pm, as the unit broke for lunch, I heard this loud buzzing sound. I, along with the rest of the cast and crew looked up and saw a helicopter in the sky which subsequently landed in the grounds. I think there were a few pangs of envy as the family and I bid our farewells and jetted off. Within 40 minutes, we were in Castle Combe.

Andy and I were approached by the BBC about doing a spin-off show featuring our two CID characters. It was to be a comedy drama set in the 1950s or sixties. I was quite keen but Andy said no. He didn't feel the comedy angle was right for him and it would have meant leaving *The Bill*. With a young family he thought it was too much of a risk. I tried to get him to change his mind; you only get one chance in this life but he was adamant. I imagine that if the series had got off the ground, it would have been a bit like *The Detectives,* starring Jasper Carrott and Robert Powell. I was disappointed, but that's life. I can't really complain that much as let's face it, I continued to have a long innings in *The Bill* which I never could have predicted at the time in this fickle industry.

Since those halcyon days, I've appeared on too many shows to mention but they include *Loose Women, Countdown,* where you record five shows in a day and Ant and Dec's *Saturday Night Takeaway,* which is probably the nearest show to Noel's original format. And the boys happily admit they were influenced by *Noel's House Party.* I appeared on their show once and while I was wandering aimlessly around the studios, I came across a young lady and asked her if she was one of the dancers. I was quite taken aback when she snapped, "No" and stomped off in a huff. Suddenly I heard a cheer and turned to see a group of backstage staff, all clearly delighted. When I asked why, they gleefully explained that the 'dancer' was actually Mel B (Scary) from The Spice Girls who had apparently been a pain all day. The idea of someone not recognising her was unthinkable but that's just me. Sometimes I get invited to Chelsea games and take Matthew along. He is beside himself when we are standing next to Frank Lampard but being totally uninterested in football, I haven't a clue who anyone is.

I never expect people to recognise me and always introduce myself but there was one time when I was at the *National TV Awards* when I thought a couple of people could have been a bit more diplomatic about not knowing who I was. I was coming down some steps at the Albert Hall when a PR approached me and asked if I would do an interview for ITV2. "Of course," I said. So I waited politely as Kelly and Jack Osbourne finished interviewing somebody else. But when they were done, I continued standing there like a lemon as they discussed who I was and whether I was worthy of their time. After a few minutes I had had enough and quietly went on my way.

One of the greatest TV experiences I have ever had was when I was the subject of *This is Your Life* in 1998. I didn't have the remotest idea that anything was going on. *The Bill* and my family did an extraordinary job of keeping it a secret. All the more amazing as I am a paid up member of the nosey parker club. The rules of the programme are very strict, dictating that if the target has an inkling, the show is cancelled. I'd have been extremely disappointed if my nosiness had put paid to one of the highlights of my life.

I didn't think it was at all suspicious when Cherry suddenly increased the number of times she attended aerobics classes from once a week to three. I just thought she was keen to get fit but little did I know that she was actually meeting with the *This is Your Life* team.

This cloak of secrecy had been going on for weeks but I was oblivious. On the day itself, I had a late call which made things awkward for Cherry. She had to somehow get herself and the kids to *The Bill*, to film some inserts without arousing my suspicions. But I wouldn't budge and Cherry was horrified when I offered to do the school run, quickly bundling the kids into the car with all her might, before I could. She suggested that maybe I should get a move on as she'd heard the traffic was bad. So as I followed her car, she took the usual exit for the school while I headed off to Merton. What I didn't know was that she then turned right back round again and went home, not setting out for Merton until a little later to ensure there was no danger of me running into them.

Laura was excited about having a day off, but Matthew hated missing school and was so conscientious that he kept checking that Cherry had definitely told the teachers he wouldn't be in that day. Neither of the kids knew until the day arrived, that they weren't going to school or why. No chances could be taken that one of them might accidentally blurt something out in front of me and ruin the plan. When Cherry did tell them, both kids agreed, "Daddy is going to kill you!"

As I wandered around the building, probably worrying everyone in case I might spot something fishy or detect an air of tension, Cherry and the kids arrived and were whisked off to *The Bill* set to film some delightful vignettes, including Matthew and Laura being banged up in a cell.

The cover story they used to disguise the *This is Your Life* film crew joining me later that day on location was a cunning one. Apparently they were filming a documentary about *The Bill* and its use of cars. Perfectly plausible but I was a bit miffed that Tom Butcher, who played PC Steve Loxton, had been asked to do the driving and not me. But when I asked why, I was told that my filming schedule was too busy.

Still afraid that I might suss what was going on, I was rushed out of the building as soon as possible. This also really bugged me. I was on two units that day and arrived far too early at the first which meant sitting in a Winnebago for ages. After lunch I was taken to the second location where the 'hit' was going to happen. By now I was not in the best of humour. This site was a dark and smelly car park in Colliers Wood, far from worthy of a slice of TV magic but a perfect example of a typical *Bill* location. The story involved Stamp, along with PC Polly Page, (Lisa Geoghan) investigating a series of thefts.

We seemed to be doing this simple scene over and over again. Unbeknown to me, the unit were waiting for the signal that Michael Aspel had arrived. I was tetchy and reminded the director it was way past time for a tea break and that I, along with the crew, who had been filming since 7.30am, were gasping. The director agreed and suggested one more take and then we could have a break

So Lisa and I got back into Sierra One for the umpteenth time. On hearing "Action" I drove up to what the coppers believe is a stolen car. Lisa was a bag of nerves as she, obviously, knew what was about to happen and put her police hat on the wrong way round. We said our pieces and I was waiting longingly to hear "Cut" as I really needed a cup of tea by now. Suddenly I noticed another police car appear, with the blues on, and start zooming towards us. I couldn't believe it. As far as I was concerned, it had ruined the shot and we would have to do it all over again. I thought I recognised Tom Butcher, but I didn't notice the grey haired geezer jump out or the red book he was clutching. Until you hear "Cut!" on set, you carry on acting so I did, trying to hide my bewilderment. I was utterly stunned when Michael Aspel stopped, whipped out his microphone and said, "Graham Cole, this is your life." Everyone began clapping and I was simply gobsmacked. I have a picture of that moment hanging in my study and you can clearly see the shock on my face.

It was mid-afternoon and the show didn't start recording until 8.30pm. So I changed into civvies and was whisked to a hotel near the studio in Teddington, South West London. My mobile phone and filofax were confiscated and I wasn't allowed to contact anyone. Those few hours were purgatory. All I kept thinking was how on earth are they going to fill a half hour show with just my life. What have I done? Other than been a jobbing actor and family man. Well, I was about to find out.

At last it was time to go. I had changed into a suit Cherry had chosen for me and headed for the studio. As I waited behind the sliding door, to walk on to the stage, I wondered who on earth was going to be there and more importantly, what would they have to say. And would I genuinely like them or had they really only been a passing acquaintance? As my life literally flashed before my eyes, I heard the sound of the film they had recorded earlier that day at Sun Hill. There were Matthew and Laura in the cells, pleading, "Free the Sun Hill two," PC Reg Hollis (Jeff Stewart) evicting Michael from custody, telling him to, "Move along sir, please." Then PC Steve Loxton (Tom Butcher) racing through the streets of Sun Hill, with Michael at his side. Finally I heard the famous *This Is Your Life* signature tune and knew it was show time. The enormous doors slid back and, with trepidation, I walked on. Fortunately there was a huge round of applause and Michael was a reassuring presence. I immediately spotted my sisters Pat and Jill and the kids Matthew and Laura. My parents were both dead by then and I felt sad that they weren't there to enjoy this special moment with me. But where was Cherry? No worries, she was next through the door to tell Michael how hard it had been to keep their crafty caper from me.

I was really pleased to see almost the entire Bill cast come on next. And I was deeply touched when Andy Paul (PC Dave Quinnan) spoke. "Graham is Mr Research. He's the unofficial fourth police advisor on the show. He probably knows more about police procedure than most police officers and that's what Graham is all about, commitment. Not just to his work but the countless numbers of charities up and down the country; to his family and all at *The Bill* too."

And Trudie Goodwin (Sergeant June Ackland) beautifully summed up my feelings towards *The Bill*, "It feels like he's always been there. Never moans like I do. But we're very lucky to have this job."

Michael opened the big Red book and began telling my story. It was a balmy summer's night and unfortunately the air conditioning had failed so it was a bit sticky up on stage, but I was too emotional to notice.

More familiar faces began streaming through the doors including former hospital colleagues; Tony Lewis who was best man at my wedding; Amy MacDonald from my panto days, who praised my singing voice. Fellow regulars on *Noel's House Party*; Tony Blackburn, who commented on my own Crinkley Bottom and comedy actress Pat Coombs, who joked, "If I was only 30 years younger." And my old mate comedian Bernie Clifton recalled a summer season in Lowestoft when, like a couple of naughty schoolboys, we played a trick on entertainer Joan Savage. We were coming to the end of the season and getting a bit restless. We knew Joan was very short sighted and didn't wear her glasses on stage. So Bernie and I got hold of a tailor's dummy, dressed it up in a suit, added a wig, placed a violin under its chin and plonked it in the orchestra pit, alongside the real life band.

It took her a few moments to pass any remarks, but finally she came off stage and witheringly said, "I've seen some line ups in my time but here you've got a piano, organ, drums and violin and you can't hear a note that violinist's playing."

Little and Large were doing summer season so couldn't attend but filmed a piece dressed in police uniform. Eddie looked rather fetching as a police woman and comically replicated the walk from *The Bill*'s closing credits.

And one of my police pals, Sergeant David Vyse, came on waving an application form for the Metropolitan Police, saying that he would very much like to have me on his force.

It was a fantastic evening and I couldn't believe all these people had gathered to pay tribute to me. At the after show party I made sure I thanked everyone and told them just how much it had meant to me. However, Cherry's abiding memory of the evening is that she wore the wrong shoes.

I love doing charity gigs and *Children in Need* is particularly close to my heart. One year Ben Richards (PC Nate Roberts), Bruce Byron (DC Terry Perkins), Daniel Flynn (Superintendent Heaton) and I impersonated the rat pack and sang Frank Sinatra's Kick in the Head. A real blast. And in 2008 I felt privileged when they asked *The Bill* to do a video to celebrate its 25th anniversary. Not only the cast but the crew gave their services free and we did a storming version of Jailhouse Rock.

Another enjoyable TV gig was doing the voiceover for the Police, Stop programmes. Producer Bill Rudgard had managed to persuade the police to let him use real police footage of various chases, seen from their viewpoint. In the early nineties it was a real coup and I was happy to be involved, as was *The Bill*. But the mechanics were far from cutting edge. I used to go to Bill's flat in Olympia, West London to record the voiceovers.

The original scripts were pretty dull and very police speak. So I began introducing my own, I like to think, witty comments, all said in an understated style. For example, there was one bizarre incident when a car in front of a police car was speeding, while towing a caravan of all things. So I described what he was doing, and the moment when the caravan suddenly disintegrated. Then I added, in a low key voice, "I think increasing his speed was a slight mistake."

When I see an episode now, it does sound a bit amateurish. And I can detect the annoyance in my voice when I describe the soft sentences some of these dangerous drivers received. They have caused a major pile-up or an elongated car chase, yet they only get a couple of points on their licence or a pathetic £50 fine. Police, Stop is shown regularly on television but sadly I don't get a penny when they are repeated.

TV game shows are great fun. I especially enjoyed appearing on *Blankety Blank* with Paul O'Grady as his alter ego Lily Savage. You always want to do your best for the contestant, whatever show you are doing, and on this occasion hope they walk away with more than just a *Blankety Blank* cheque book and pen. Liz Dawn, who played Vera Duckworth in *Coronation Street* had been selected to help the contestant in the final round, and was asked to add a word after "bell." For some reason she said "end" and we all collapsed into fits of laughter. Paul stuck a hankie in his mouth to try to stop laughing but in the end it was hopeless and they had to stop filming. It took us all a good 20 minutes to recover. Having finally regained her composure, when filming resumed, Liz offered the more sensible "ringer."

Another giggler is the delightful Fern Britton who at the time co-presented *This Morning*. I was on the show for a general chat and there was an upcoming feature about health checks. Fern asked me whether I had an exercise routine? Quick as a flash I replied, "Would regular exercise with the wife count?" Fern dissolved and unable to speak, I had to do the next link.

But when invited on to a celebrity edition of *The Weakest Link*, I mentally pumped myself up to face the indomitable Anne Robinson. I think I got away lightly as she only teased me about Stamp's undoubtedly pathetic love life. Giving me one of her stares she snarled, "Tony Stamp's been very unlucky in love and now he's hooked up with June. What's that all about?" I couldn't resist by replying, "But I thought of you all the time Anne," which I think she liked.

It was great fun but a very long day. We started filming at three in the afternoon and didn't finish until nine at night. While the contestants were writing the names on the board, Anne would disappear for about 20 minutes. I think she was being given some clever quips by the writers. I came a respectable third. I was elbowed out by some dapper bloke from *The Archers*.

## CHAPTER ELEVEN

# Encore

As my story so far, draws to a close, I still can't believe my luck. I've had the most wonderful life; a fantastic job for longer than any actor has the right to think possible and a smashing wife and family. And my good fortune has enabled me to give something back through my charity work. Unfortunately, celebrities jumping on the charity bandwagon has become something of a cliché in this jaded 21st century of ours.

But I can honestly say, hand on heart, that being able to make a difference, no matter how small, is a precious thing. Personally, I would prefer to use whatever 'celebrity kudos' I had for good causes rather than getting the best seat in a fancy restaurant. Though admittedly it can sometimes come in handy.

Once, Matthew and I were queuing up to get into the Capital Radio Café in Leicester Square. Tired of waiting Matthew pleaded, "Pleeeeease can I go and tell them who you are dad?" But I refused. "If I have to tell them who I am, then what's the point?" Ironically, within 30 seconds a burly security man appeared and ushered us in. But I would never dream of demanding, "Don't you know who I am?" And anyway, what if they didn't? I would have felt duly shamefaced.

Interestingly enough, Matthew must have taken a bit of notice of his old Dad. On his 20th birthday, we arranged to meet up with him and some of his mates at London's Hard Rock Café. As usual, I was running late due to work and as I walked towards their table, I could see that his friends weren't sure why Graham Cole from *The Bill* was coming towards them. It turned out that although Matthew had told them I worked on *The Bill*, they had assumed it was as a cameraman or director, not PC Tony Stamp. And he had never bothered to put them straight. I hope it was due to modesty rather than embarrassment that he hadn't let the cat out of the bag.

Not wishing to blow my own trumpet, charity work genuinely takes up a lot of my spare time. In 2008 alone I did 84 charity gigs and loved every minute. I mainly support children's charities because I feel I've never really grown up and therefore maybe, I understand a little better where the kids are coming from. But it's also because children cannot speak up for or defend themselves.

Understandably, I have also been heavily involved with a number of police charities that have contacted me over the years, having obviously seen me in *The Bill*. The warm welcome I get when I turn up to any of these events is truly humbling. And when they heard that I was leaving *The Bill*, I was touched when they all contacted me hoping I would carry on the good work.

Recently I was thrilled when Childline and the NSPCC, who work together a lot, inducted me into their Hall of Fame. It was in recognition of the work I have done over the past 20 years, raising a considerable amount of money for one of my favourite charities. The presentation took place at the House of Commons and I cannot put into words just how proud I felt.

I particularly love being the auctioneer at a charity auction. It's great fun although some of the items on offer can be a little bizarre. Why anyone would want to buy the underpants Rhys Ifans wore in the film *Notting Hill* is beyond me. Although, in this case, at least they were tastefully framed.

But when I was invited to be the figure head for an anti-bullying campaign, I never dreamt that this was an issue close to home. I knew bullying was endemic; it doesn't just happen at school but also in the workplace and I wanted to help. It never occurred to me that someone in my own family might be a victim Now, I am a great believer that charity begins at home so imagine my horror when I discovered that my own daughter, Laura, was being bullied at school. And that it had been going on for some time.

My children have very different characters. While Matthew is a high flier, who studied law at university, Laura leans towards creativity and has shown a real flair for acting. Like many actors, I am cautious about my child following in my footsteps. Acting is such a hit and miss profession, often more reliant on luck than talent. And it can be incredibly cruel. You need a thick skin to protect yourself from the endless rejections that are part of any actor's life, no matter how successful. And it's not just about getting that job. You have to keep on getting the job time and time again or, in my case, hold on to it. There are always ambitious, younger wannabes behind you, snapping at your heels. Like any good parent I want to protect Laura and yet at the same time, I can't help thinking who am I to dash her dreams?

School is a place that should prepare you for the harsh realities of the outside world but I never thought Laura would face its brutality at such a young age. Cherry and I had been unable to get Laura into our first choice of secondary school. So despite having settled in well at our second choice, we believed that our original choice, Langley Girls in Beckenham, was still the better school. And we wouldn't give up trying to get Laura in. We felt we owed it to Laura to give her the best possible start in life. In hindsight I wish we had left well alone. After 18 months of sitting through a series of tribunals, we were over the moon when our wish was granted and a place was found at our preferred choice of school. And so began years of misery for our beloved daughter.

From the day she arrived Laura was targeted. As an all girls' school, it didn't help that by the time she arrived, most of the pupils had formed their own cliques, and this latecomer wasn't welcome to join any of them.

As a society we seem to assume that the victims of bullying are usually fat or plain with thick rimmed glasses and spots. But that is rarely the case. It can be the simplest thing that sparks off some sort of resentment. In Laura's case, just being tall for her age, keen on drama and playing the clarinet, seems to have really annoyed a spiteful few. And it probably didn't help that, 'Her dad was on the telly.' Laura became a pariah. She was always chosen last for any team sports. And no one would sit next to her in assembly. Basically she was sent to Coventry on a daily basis. She had the odd friend but they too were too scared to stand up to the bullies.

Laura suffered in silence. She never said a word to either Cherry or I. She now says that she didn't want to worry us and anyway, it wouldn't have made a scrap of difference. Sadly, as we were to find out, she was right about that. Even when we noticed her grades were slipping, she remained resolutely silent.

It was only when I mentioned that I was getting involved with an anti-bullying campaign, that she finally blurted it all out. By this time she was 13 and the bullying had been going on quite a while. I couldn't believe what I was hearing. How could they do that to my little girl? Why hadn't the school tried to put a stop to it? Immediately, Cherry and I made an appointment to see Laura's Head of Year. We listened as the head droned on about how there was no such thing as bullying in this school. "We take great pride in that, Mr and Mrs Cole. Such behaviour will not be tolerated. We carefully follow the anti-bullying code. Have you heard of it at all?"

By now I was fuming. She didn't even have the grace to acknowledge there was a problem. And all this time neither she nor her fellow teachers had noticed that Laura was in such distress and that the quality of her work had deteriorated. Here was my cue to fight back. I sat up straight and in my best theatrical voice, smugly replied, "Heard of it? Perhaps if you had taken the time to look a little more closely at that poster behind you, exhibiting the code, you might have noticed my name is at the bottom."

She was mortified and promised to keep an eye on Laura. But when she returned to class, this incompetent head foolishly announced that Laura was being bullied and it's probably by one of you. Which only made the situation worse as now it was clear that Laura was also a tell tale. The only solution the school came up with was to issue her with a kind of credit card which she was to give to a teacher when she was being bullied; she would then be sent to see the Head of Year. But they never did anything concrete about it.

After she had left school Laura found the courage to accompany me when I was doing the rounds, drumming up publicity for the anti-bullying campaign and joined me on *GMTV*, among others. At least by now she had left school and felt she could speak out freely, in the hope of helping others. Not long after, Laura and I were at the Grosvenor House for a charity event in aid of Great Ormond Street Hospital when one of the nurses approached us. "I went to that school and I too was bullied and even now when Sister speaks to me in a disapproving tone, I revert right back to that scared 14-year-old. I just wanted to say thank you for speaking out."

During that period I was so angry that I bought a punch bag and knocked the living daylights out of it. A few years later, I was on the panel of a Childline conference, alongside Esther Rantzen, a couple of government ministers and a bunch of education experts. When I relayed my story, saying that punching the bag had really helped with my anger, one of the education bods piped up, "That's hardly setting a good example is it?" He really didn't get it did he? "Surely," I retorted, "it's better than going up the school and thumping the teachers?" That shut him up.

I am enormously proud of both of my children who, like me, are keen to give something back. Matthew has volunteered as a counsellor for Childline and Laura is considering becoming a police support officer. While Laura attends church along with Cherry and I, Matthew, like me when I was around his age, attends a youth group called Hill Song who meet in London theatres with rock music groups and guest speakers. However, to this day, I still feel huge guilt about helping others and yet not being able to help my own daughter.

Probably the charity I am proudest to be associated with is The Grand Order of Water Rats. When I was initially approached, by the prolific guitarist Bert Weedon, I was genuinely overcome; especially when he said, "I think you would make a wonderful Water Rat." I had heard of the Water Rats but never dreamt I would be invited to become one.

The Grand Order of Water Rats is the entertainment industry's very own charity. Founded in 1889, it began life as a racing syndicate, made up of a group of music hall performers. Once, on spotting their horse, which was getting soaking wet in the rain, a driver remarked that it looked more like, "a drowned water rat than a race horse." So when the syndicate decided to found their own charity, to help out those less fortunate in the business than themselves, they opted to be known as The Grand Order of Water Rats. Especially apt as "rats" spelt backwards, becomes "star."

In spite of jumping at the chance to join, that was only the beginning; there remained a strict, elaborate process to be gone through. Once Bert submitted my name, research had to be done to see if I was truly worthy. If found to be a suitable candidate, a member, on this occasion Bert himself, had to stand up and argue why someone like Graham Cole should be allowed to join. The committee would then vote "Yay" or "Nay."

Anyone who is anyone in showbiz is a member including Frank Carson, Barry Cryer, Paul Daniels, Brian May, Nicholas Parsons, Engelbert Humperdink, Derek Martin (Charlie in *EastEnders*), Jimmy Perry, Bernie Clifton and Lionel Blair. Along with a few powerful showbiz agents. Former members included comic Les Dawson, singer Howard Keel and and comedy legend Tommy Cooper. Membership is strictly limited to so I was on tenterhooks waiting to see if my application would be accepted. So when I heard that I had been accepted, I couldn't contain my delight. It was just such an honour.

The Water Rats raise money by putting on shows, lunches and dinners and the object is to 'assist members of the theatrical profession, or their dependents who, due to illness or old age have fallen on hard times.' Additional funds go to other charities and good causes such as hospitals and benevolent funds like Brinsworth House in Twickenham, South West London, the retirement home for former performers. DJ Alan Freeman, actress Thora Hird and comic Charlie Drake all ended their days there.

Now you've probably noticed that all the members are men. That's because the ladies also have their own charitable organisation called The Grand Order of Lady Ratlings which was founded in 1929. Cherry is a member along with luminaries such as Ruth Madoc, Dame Vera Lynn and Barbara Windsor.

The walls of the Water Rats headquarters in King's Cross are plastered with showbiz memorabilia including one of Charlie Chaplin's canes and his little black hat plus a fez owned by the great Tommy Cooper. We have our very own pub downstairs and young bands often play there in the hope that agents will spot them. Oasis did a gig there before they were famous.

Having been allowed to join, I was stunned but delighted when I was elected King Rat in 2009. My role is a bit like that of the chairman of a company except that I get to wear an amazing blue collar, similar to a mayor's chain of office. It is very big and quite heavy as it is covered in small gold plaques with the names of past King Rats engraved on them. My duties include presiding over meetings, which we hold every fortnight, helping to decide the year's calendar of events, hearing what some members are up to and sanctioning new members. I also have the power to award the jester award for a good joke and an egg for a bad one. And once in a while I get to offer my services as a song and dance man at a few of the Water Rats shows.

I also handle requests not only from current members but also relatives of former Water Rats, like Lois Laurel, daughter of Stan Laurel of Laurel and Hardy fame. Michael Levy who plays the seen but rarely heard milkman in *EastEnders*, is a member of the Laurel and Hardy Association. Lois contacted him because while moving house she had lost her father's Water Rat pin. It had meant so much to him that she was devastated. Being King Rat I had to sanction our sending a new one, which of course I was more than happy to do.

My faith remains another constant in my life and is enormously important to me. Yet being a Christian has become distinctly unfashionable; in the words of Radio Two presenter Jeremy Vine, "It has become socially unacceptable." Admittedly, there have been times, as an actor, when I have struggled with the demands of a role because of my beliefs. For example, I thought long and hard about accepting the role of Pontius Pilate in *Jesus Christ Superstar*. I did some research and found that he really did try to stop Jesus being crucified. And after all it is one hell of a story which Tim Rice and Andrew Lloyd Webber managed to make truly accessible to the masses. No harm in that. There are also some great tunes.

My beliefs have helped me through some of the worst times in my life. Losing Dad, Pat and of course, my Mum, back in 1991. Mum was never that active but then she did have some genuine health problems, including high blood pressure for most of her life. She was one of those people whose social life revolved around trips to the doctor and most of the time she was on at least six tablets a day. After Dad died she was happy enough to stay in the Harlow house but as the years wore on and she became less and less mobile, it was far too big for her. But mum was a stubborn old bird. Even after suffering a series of mini strokes she refused to move. She could no longer do the stairs which were very steep and had her bed set up in the lounge but of course, the toilet was still upstairs. No matter how much Pat, Jill and I pleaded that it was time to move, she wouldn't hear of it. Finally yet another stroke left her so incapacitated that she was taken into hospital.

We had booked a family holiday to Canada and I was hesitant to leave Mum. She was now semi-paralysed and speech was hard but she painstakingly managed to make it clear that she would be fine and we were to go off on our holiday.

We were only gone a few days when I got the call from my sister Jill telling me that Mum had died. I cried and cried and was and still am eaten up with guilt that I wasn't there to say goodbye. People try to comfort you by saying it was what she wanted but how do they or I really know? At times she wasn't the easiest of people and sometimes she could be downright difficult, especially when it came to Cherry, but she was my Mum and she gave me the best start any kid could have by loving me unconditionally. I like to imagine her and Dad up there in Heaven and, as usual, he is waiting on her hand and foot.

My faith had already been seriously tested when Cherry was so ill during both her pregnancies but was tested, once again, when she was involved in a serious accident. About seven years ago we were outside Selfridges, on London's Oxford Street and standing by a zebra crossing waiting to cross the road. Cherry was holding Laura's hand when all of sudden I watched in what seemed like slow motion as Cherry was scooped up by a car, landing on the bonnet, still holding Laura's hand then dumped on the road when the car came to a screeching halt. Everyone started screaming and as I rushed over, I was consumed with dread, convinced she was dead. Once again those feelings of life being unbearable without her swept over me. The driver, who was a young girl who had just passed her test, had apparently been looking over at me and simply didn't see Cherry. Fortunately, she was quick to stop and dashed out to help Cherry. She was alive, thank God, but all she kept saying was that she couldn't feel her legs. As we waited for the ambulance, I tried to comfort both Cherry and the kids, Matthew and Laura. Both, unsurprisingly, were in floods of tears, having witnessed their Mum nearly being killed. Inevitably a crowd gathered round and started taking photos. We were all in shock and although I couldn't believe people's insensitivity, especially as all you could hear was, "It's that bloke off *The Bill*," at the same time I knew this goes with the territory. Matthew, on the other hand, was getting increasingly angry, screaming, "Leave her alone, that's my Mum!"

Within minutes a paramedic arrived on a motorbike and put a collar around Cherry's neck. But she still kept on saying, "I can't feel my legs." Every time I heard it, I felt sick. As I tried to keep her calm, I kept wishing it had been me who had been hit; I couldn't bear the thought of her being crippled. When the ambulance arrived the paramedics put an oxygen mask on Cherry's face, gently carried her onto a board and she and Matthew were whisked away to University College London Hospital while Laura and I followed in the car. Cherry always says that Matthew was amazing that day. Calm and collected, telling her everything was going to be alright. A wise head on some very young shoulders.

And what happened next was truly a miracle. Cherry was given an MRI scan which was hard for her as she is claustrophobic. But obviously the doctors had to see if any internal damage had been done. I think that was probably the longest half an hour of my life as we waited for the results. Unbelievably there was nothing broken and gradually the feeling in her legs began to come back. She was severely bruised and her legs had swollen up to three times their normal size. After barely four hours Cherry was able to walk out of the hospital on crutches. The doctor said that if she had been facing towards the car, it would have been a lot, lot worse Bed rest and weeks of physiotherapy literally got her back on her feet. But sadly the accident seems to have brought on arthritis which is incredibly painful but I thank God every day that she is still here. I have never once thought about turning my back on God. I truly believe faith is not worth having if it is not regularly put to the test. I suppose it's like supporting a football team that always wins; how hard is that?

Unbelievably, the driver later attempted to sue us for "stress." She claimed Cherry stepped off the kerb but after admitting she had been looking at me instead of the road, the case was dropped.

I always knew that one day my time at *The Bill* would come to an end but it was still a horrible shock when it actually happened. I suppose that's the eternal optimist in me. With the economic downturn really biting, it is sad but true, that TV drama, which is very expensive, would be hardest hit. And understandably *The Bill* has had to tighten its belt, cutting back the number of episodes produced annually. Along with the number of cast and crew. But I didn't think that would include me. Not yet anyway.

Over the years I have witnessed a plethora of actors being shown the door. Jon Iles, who played dashing DC Mike Dashwood and was a great party organiser at *The Bill*, found out during his lunch break from his agent, that his contract wasn't being renewed. Hugh Ellis, the son of Peter Ellis who played Superintendent Charles Brownlow (but in real-life wasn't remotely like stern Brownlow) was called in and told that Brownlow was leaving but he wasn't to tell his dad. And poor Eric Richard, who had played iconic Sergeant Bob Cryer for 17 years found out he was departing when he saw it splashed all over the tabloid newspapers.

Lesser known character PC Natasha Williams, played by Delia French, was undercover as a drugs mule when she went upstairs and never came down. A bit like that classic moment in *Crossroads* when Benny went to get a spanner and did not return for six months. But at least he came back! Trudie Goodwin decided to leave when her character June Ackland was raped by a 14-year-old boy. The story simply didn't ring true.

So I always believed that when the time came, my exit would be different. After all, I had been playing PC Tony Stamp for a quarter of a century. Surely an achievement like that deserved something spectacular or at least a happy ending?

About three weeks before I was told my contract wasn't being renewed, *The Bill* building was buzzing about the changes that were afoot. The show was already being shot in High Definition which we were all excited about but now the opening credits and the music were getting a makeover. And despite the number of episodes being cut from two a week to one, it would be broadcast post watershed, i.e. after 9pm. This meant its contents could be grittier and increasingly action packed; basically more adult.

But I hoped this didn't mean any bad language. Much as I love working in television, I wish there wasn't quite so much bad language. And I don't think that has anything to do with my religious beliefs. I know I probably sound like Victor Meldrew but I actually think it's a sign of lazy writing. You can imply certain words with a look rather than relying on endless profane exclamations. If you do your job right as an actor the audience will know what you are thinking. When Stamp witnesses DC Viv Martella being shot dead in *The Bill*, he simply mutters, "Oh, sh….," far more effective. And the audience knows what he means.

I was genuinely excited as I have always embraced change. Naively perhaps it never occurred to me that this new Bill could mean the beginning of the end for old Bill like Stamp.

The day I found out I wasn't part of this new Bill was Wednesday 27th May. I was on my way back from my brother-in-law Doug's funeral. He had been married to my late sister Pat. I was driving home with Laura when the phone rang. It was series producer Tim Key's PA informing me that the screening for all cast and crew of the first episode in the new format was now being shown at base tomorrow rather than a pub as originally planned. Okay fine. 20 minutes later the phone rang and it was the PA again, "Tim would like you to come in earlier for a meeting at 4pm." As the screening was not until 7pm, I asked why. She either didn't know or couldn't say but something told me it wasn't good news. A cold feeling came over me as I turned to Laura and said, "I think this is the end of Tony Stamp." I rang the PA back and insisted that Tim call me when he was out of his meeting. If I'm honest and now with the benefit of hindsight I should've realised things weren't right and hadn't been for quite a while. I hadn't had any big episodes for nearly a year; there were weeks when I was hardly doing any filming at all. Just the odd scene where me and my great mate John Bowler were shuffling papers in the background. But then that wasn't that unusual on *The Bill*. Everyone gets their 15 minutes and as there were usually over 25 cast members, this sometimes took a long time.

Half an hour later the phone rang and this time it was Tim. "Graham, I really don't want to do this on the phone," he said, "I would far rather talk to you face to face tomorrow." But I insisted that I was an adult and I would prefer to hear what I had already guessed by now, rather than have a sleepless night, worrying. So I calmly asked, "Is it what I think it is?" and he replied "Yes, I'm afraid we are not renewing your contract in July." As I began to take it in, I told him, "I too don't want to talk anymore on the phone. Now that I know what it is I can deal with it. I'll see you tomorrow at 4pm." It all felt very odd. The only way I can explain it is that it was like someone telling you that your favourite uncle had died. Stamp was no more.

I waited before I got home to tell Cherry. She knew something was wrong the moment Laura and I walked through the door. She could see it on our faces. Laura's was tear-stained and I was white as a sheet. As always she was reassuring. After all, we both knew this day would come; it was time for change etc. All the platitudes I desperately needed to hear.

Not once have I ever not wanted to go into work since I started at *The Bill* and this day was no different. I knew what was coming and I just hoped that I and Stamp would be treated with some respect. At that stage nobody else knew and as I made my way to Tim's office, I bumped into Andrew Lancel, who plays DI Neil Manson. He and I have always got on well and when I told him where I was going he joked, "So this is it then, is it?" "Well, funnily enough...." and I told him. He was shocked and kept saying he couldn't believe it.

Now as I sat opposite Tim in his office, he kept apologising for being the bearer of bad news. "I'm so sorry Graham but as you can see we've changed the format quite considerably and your contract is coming up for renewal and it was felt that we've taken Stamp as far as he can go..." As an actor you hear that phrase a lot, "We've taken your character as far as it can go" and I don't particularly like it. I suppose it's better than being told you're too old or too grey or too fat, less personal. After talking for about 20 minutes about Stamp's exit storyline, I put Tim, who I could see was finding this very hard, out of his misery and left.

I was then due to see the executive producer Jonathan Young at 6pm and had every intention of staying for the screening so I went back to my dressing room. Within minutes there was a knock at the door and there was my mate John Bowler asking, "Is it true then?" He was swiftly followed by Andrew and a succession of actors who all couldn't believe what they had heard and said how much they would miss me. I was truly touched. Last but certainly not least was Alex Walkinshaw, Sergeant Dale Smith, who has since been promoted to inspector. And if there is one person I am happy to pass the asp (the telescopic baton) on to it is Alex. Neither of us said anything for ages but just hugged and hugged.

When I saw Jonathan later that day, he pretty much said the same as Tim except that he wasn't sure it was the right decision to which I replied, "Well you'd better make your mind up quick as I'll be well gone by November." To which we both laughed. He even hinted that there might be the odd guest appearance by Stamp but I think he was just being polite. I might return if Alex's character Smithy is buried under a pile of scaffolding, dying and he and Stamp could reminisce about old times as they wait for help.

Jonathan, just like Tim, was very kind about Stamp but I sensed there was an urgency about getting rid of Stamp as soon as possible in case he tainted the new Bill. That evening I walked into the screening and watched the promos that had been made to promote the new Bill. Unsurprisingly, despite having participated in the filming of these, I wasn't in any of them. Then the episode started and I was blown away by the new format and how exciting it was. And then it hit me. I wasn't going to be a part of this new-look Bill. My time as a regular in one of the most successful shows on British television was over. As these thoughts raced through my head, I got a text from Cherry to say that Matthew, who lives and works in the City, had come home to be there for me. As I read it, the tears started to flow, not just for me and what I was losing but for PC Tony Stamp who was now pretty much dead and buried. I was very upset. I began to make my excuses and leave but as I walked away I heard Andrew's voice shouting, "I give you Graham Cole" and the cast burst into applause as I faded into the night.

That evening Cherry, Laura and Matthew and I shed a lot of tears. Laura was particularly upset at the prospect of never seeing PC Tony Stamp again. And Cherry hates the thought of going back to those days when I was off on tour, here there and everywhere. If I have to then so be it but she can't possibly come with me anymore, she's just not up to it.

Now I've said before that my big gob soon got me into a fair share of trouble over the years. I have always had a very good relationship with the Stampers Fan Club who are, as the name suggests, fans of PC Tony Stamp. It was a week later but still only *The Bill* and my immediate family knew that I was going. The press office had asked how I wanted to handle this and suggested a statement saying I was leaving by mutual agreement. But I wasn't keen as it simply wasn't true. And as I had started writing this book, I was determined to be truthful. It hurts but sometimes the truth does that. The press office was so worried about my state of mind that they rang my agent, Lesley Duff, to check I was okay. I think they thought I might do a Jeff Stewart. As if. I was definitely hurt and upset but my family and my faith has always given me an inner strength to enable me to get through anything life can throw at me. Yes, even losing a job I loved.

In my naivety I decided to let the Stampers know. I felt that they deserved to be told directly by me, not hear it second hand, but I never dreamed that they would leak it to the press. This is what I wrote in an email to Glen Quigley who organises the Stampers:

"How do I tell you this? The management have decided that PC Tony Stamp will not be a part of the new nine o'clock show. I cannot tell you how disappointed and disregarded I feel. Tony has been a wonderful character to play. They say he doesn't fit into the new 'dynamic', so I have to be out before the big relaunch in November.

"I will launch the new nine o'clock format but then they don't want anything negative within the new show. So poor old Tony will be sent to training school, with the door left open for odd episodes."

As you can detect, I was still raw. I had a nice reply from Glen saying how shocked he was and I didn't think too much about it. That is until I got a call from my agent Lesley saying *The Bill* press office had contacted her after spotting the story of my departure on something called Digital Spy. Now I had never heard of Digital Spy but apparently it is an on-line gossip site and there, in all its glory was the story of my leaving.

Headed: 'PC Tony Stamped out of *The Bill*,' which I have to admit was quite clever, it broke the story as follows:

'*The Bill*'s current longest-serving character PC Tony Stamp has been axed from the series after nearly 22 years [25 actually] Digital Spy can confirm. Graham, who made his first appearance as Tony in September 1987, [wrong again] will leave the long-running series later this year after producers decided that the police officer "doesn't fit" the show's new "dynamic".'

It then went on to reproduce my email, word for word. I was stunned and disappointed and quickly told Glen how I felt. He desperately tried to get it taken off the site but it was too late as the story was out there and a number of publications had inevitably spotted it. *The Bill* press office went into damage limitation mode, hastily issuing a statement from me:

"I have had a wonderful time patrolling the streets of Sun Hill and of course, I'm sad to leave. Tony has been a big part of my life for a long time, but I'm looking forward to seeking out some new challenges and enjoying life outside the nick."

Jonathan Young also gave a quote, "Graham is a much-loved and admired member of cast. He has contributed an enormous amount to *The Bill* and we are grateful for his enthusiasm and support over the years. PC Tony Stamp leaves an amazing legacy."

True enough. Maybe it wasn't exactly the way I would have wanted the news to get out but then again, I would rather people knew the truth, that my contract hadn't been renewed. It's one of the hazards of being an actor and although I was very down about it at first, I quickly accepted that things move on and I have had a fantastic innings. The next day the story was splashed all over the tabloids. The *Daily Mirror* had my face on the front page and headlined their story 'Stamp's Copped It.' And the *Daily Mail* went straight for the jugular, 'PC Stamp axed from *The Bill* after

22 years for being too old.' Thanks.

At least the *TV Times* was a little kinder. 'Fans in uproar as Graham Cole's PC Stamp gets the boot from *The Bill*,' and asked their readers to write in if they thought the producers had made the wrong call. Even Fern Britton and Phil Schofield on *This Morning* mentioned how cross they were at what had happened. In fact Phil has been brilliant and really supportive of me for which I am very grateful. I have been bombarded by emails and letters from members of the public saying how much they are going to miss Stamp and wishing me well which has been incredibly humbling and comforting. Several former cast members have contacted me, including my mate Trudie Goodwin who rings me every week, even though she is currently on tour with a play, saying that there's plenty of life out there. I know she's right.

As I say, my faith has helped me stay strong throughout many difficult periods in my life and despite losing a job I love, that remains the case. I can honestly say that within two weeks of learning my fate, I had come to terms with it and I'm now excited about the future.

The week after learning I was being dropped, I attended Alex Walkinshaw's wedding. Stars of *The Bill* old and new were there including Mark Wingett, who was convinced that being given such short notice was illegal. But how could I ever say anything bad about *The Bill* itself? It is an awesome machine with an amazing cast and crew behind it. I know it will continue to be a huge success and I can only say how proud I am to have been such an integral part for so long.

But that doesn't mean I'm not able to voice my own personal disappointment at the way I – and Stamp – were allowed to leave after so many years of loyalty. I'm not saying there should have been a fanfare or high drama but I did think my final scenes were somewhat low-key, almost as if they wanted to pretend it wasn't really happening which I suppose is the case. I'm sure they wished I could just go and go quickly.

For about eight weeks after I was sacked, I heard nothing, not a word from *The Bill*. Then one Friday I got a phone call asking me to have lunch with my agent Lesley and series producer Tim. On that very morning, two pages of script had arrived, not a whole script, just two pages. In it Stamp says "This is my 47th dead body and I always promised myself when it got to 50 that would be it." So I thought that was it, my last lines. The end after 25 years. But actually it was a build up scene for an episode before my last one.

Then when I was in the building, I learned about two other scripts I was supposed to be in. When I asked about them, I was told one wasn't finished and that the other had been sent out to me. They gave me a copy and it was literally Stamp's goodbye. I went to my dressing room and read of Stamp's fate. If you happen to have seen it by now you'll probably agree that it is quite a nice farewell, but I must confess I would have liked to have been more heavily featured in my last story.

Basically, we're in a riot situation and Stamp is being what he's good at which is the community cop. There's a couple who he befriends and he's trying to placate them as their front door has been flattened by cops by mistake. Finally Stamp says to Smithy that he's applied to police driving school to teach coppers how to drive so we learn how he's leaving Sun Hill. Right at the end, he gets into the car and the radio goes but Stamp realises he can't answer it because he's not a member of the Sun Hill team any more. I know how he feels.

As I say, it's all quite nice but I can't help but feel disappointed that the final episode Stamp is in, after a quarter of a century in *The Bill*, doesn't actually feature him as such. It's just a few scenes here and there and that's it, all over for good. He'll probably never be mentioned again! To be honest, I think the show's moved on to what they want it to be and Stamp was never going to be a part of that. I'm pretty sure they'd made up their minds about this some time ago and nothing I could have said or done would have changed that.

It hit home how different the new-look *Bill* is when I was filming the scene in which Stamp finds his 47th body. He and some other coppers are treading all over the crime scene which I did point out, only to get some old fashioned looks as if to say, "So?" And when some of the other actors and I later talked about it in the Winnebago, even they were saying things like, "But it's only television." Well to me, what made *The Bill* stand out was that it was as close to real life policing as possible, almost fly-on-the-wall at times. And as soon as you move away from that, as soon as the actors don't act like policemen, you lose the essence of the show. We'd always been very, very good on *The Bill* with all that procedural stuff that real coppers have to do. It's a really important part of their job which is why they watched it too, I suspect.

In my heart I think the powers that be should have called the show something else, maybe The New Bill, so that the audience don't feel that what they're tuning into is what they've been watching for the past 25 years. It's new, exciting, different and I would have loved to have been a part of it but it was not to be. The last time I was in the building I experienced a mixture of emotions. There are a lot of people there who I've known for years and it was tough leaving them behind. On the other hand, I felt like an outsider as well. The lads were talking about up coming scripts and storylines but I realised I wasn't one of the lads so it was a relief to finish up and go.

What hurts the most is being given just two months notice that Stamp was being axed, but perhaps it was something to do with the fact that the management were under great pressure to change the format of the show. Two months simply isn't enough time to get everything in order when all you've been used to for the past 20-odd years is a particular job.

Obviously I'm a jobbing actor and nothing can ever be taken for granted. But surely they could have taken me aside and, said, "We don't really think your character has anywhere to go and we won't be renewing your contract in six months time." I would have been shocked and upset but at least I could have sorted myself out financially. Of course we earn good money in television but when your job ends you don't get any redundancy money, even if you've done the same job, like I have, for more than two decades.

So when you're out, that's it, you're on your own which is why I think it would have been fairer to give me – and others in my position – a decent notice period. For instance, I was sacked in the middle of June when casting for the panto season is organised in April! That significantly reduced my chances of getting a panto job for Christmas 2009.

More worrying to me than the loss of my actual job was my family and how they'd deal with this huge change in our lives. I have a wonderful agent and within days, she had offers coming in for me, some of which I'm still in talks about and others I've accepted. For instance, in the summer, while waiting to hear about my departure scenes from *The Bill*, I filmed the gameshow *A Hole in the Wall* with Anton du Beck. But I was concerned how my loved ones would adapt to the change in our lifestyles as I go back to being a jobbing actor once more and all the uncertainty that entails.

My immediate biggest worry, on hearing that I was to go, was that we might lose our lovely family house. Ironically, we never ever took any chances financially and every time we moved it was because we had to. As I've already mentioned, there was one house that Cherry really loved when the kids were quite young but we decided we couldn't afford it because I'd been in *The Bill* six years and had no inkling how much longer it would last. I'm not convinced Cherry has quite forgiven me, even now. But when Cherry heard about this house a few years ago, we decided to take the plunge. I felt that after all these years, my loyal wife deserved her dream home and I didn't want another house she had her heart set on to slip through our fingers. It's a decision we could yet live to regret, although I do hope not.

The thought of having to give up what is basically my thank you to Cherry for what she has had to contend with over the years is heartbreaking. I know in the current economic climate some would say I have been foolish by taking out a large mortgage. But actors are dreamers and I have always wanted to make Cherry's dreams come true. And to thank the entire family for what they have had to put up with, what with my being away so much, appearing in summer seasons and provincial theatre all over the country. Then there were the long hours on *The Bill*, combined with the constant intrusion when we were out and about as a family. They've never once complained and done nothing but support me.

Of course it was all part of the job but sometimes it could get a little bit nasty. Once we were all at Gatwick Airport, about to fly off to Spain. Cherry was recovering from pleurisy and needed a complete rest. We were having lunch and I was cutting up a burger for Laura when I was tapped on the shoulder by an autograph hunter. Amiably, I explained, "I'll be with you in a minute, just need to finish doing this." Well he went mad and began ranting for a full 10 minutes about how I'd be nobody without the likes of him and certainly wouldn't be able to afford to take my family on "fancy holidays." When he finally finished I told him to shut up, turned around and carried on having my lunch. You can't argue with people like that but if it hadn't been for the kids I probably would have punched his lights out.

But he was right about one thing. Without *The Bill*, there are so many people I would never have met, so many things I wouldn't have done and so many places I wouldn't have got the chance to visit. One of my favourites is Australia where *The Bill* is a big hit. Shown on ABC, their equivalent of the BBC, they used to join the half-hour episodes together and show them on a Saturday night. It was odd watching episodes squeezed together in that way as that was not the original intention. They had been made weeks apart, and it really showed. It also highlighted those actors who regularly gave their all. And those who just turned up to deliver their lines without very much thought.

Older Bill episodes are screened on UKTV, the equivalent of the Gold channel. Tony Iffland is the Chief Executive and has invited the family and me over a few times. When UKTV was being launched in New Zealand, Tony invited me to do a publicity tour of both Australia and New Zealand. It was at very short notice but luckily *The Bill* managed to rejig my schedule so that I could go.

It was a 24 hour flight and the moment I stepped off the plane, I was set to work. And that's the way I like it. I gave loads of interviews to radio, TV, newspaper and magazines, met competition winners and even posed with a police car for some pictures down at Auckland docks. Everywhere I went, I was greeted by crowds of fans of *The Bill*.

Then we were whisked off to Sydney. Tony, a Rolf Harris lookey-likey, is brilliant at making sure Cherry and the kids are well looked after, rightly believing that if I know they are happy then I am too. UKTV had asked me to bring over a signed photo of Stamp in uniform. I had chosen one of my favourites which features Stamp standing by the river with Canary Wharf in the background. A wonderful iconic shot of both Stamp and modern London.

We were on our way to Planet Hollywood to present the picture and already feeling rather grand in this Mercedes with blacked out windows. Tony's phone rang and I heard him mention "trouble." When he finished the call he told me that there was some crowd trouble at Planet Hollywood and the police had asked if we would drive around the block a few times until they had everything under control.

"Is there some kind of riot going on?" I asked in all innocence. "No, no, no," he replied, "there's a large crowd waiting to see you." I couldn't believe it. But it was true. When we finally pulled up it was like a Hollywood premiere. There were people everywhere, cheering and shouting my name and Stamp's, cameras flashing and the police holding back the crowd. I felt like a bona fide film star. I kept thinking this is what it must be like to be Tom Cruise. Tony swears he hadn't tipped anyone off so I have no idea how they knew I was going to be there. But I'm mighty glad they did. I'm looking forward to taking my memoirs to Australia and meeting my Aussie fans once again. Stamp will be on screens down under for some time to come and it will be wonderful to get some sunshine and talk about my character to die hard *Bill* supporters.

And what about PC Tony Stamp? What does the future

hold for the soft-hearted area car driver? I quite like the idea of him being sent to the police driving school to develop the next generation of coppers. I'm sure he'll do well and show them what real police driving is all about. And after retiring, he wouldn't go down the usual route and turn into a run of the mill security guard; I see him more as a private detective. In his mind's eye he would probably liken himself to Jim Rockford or Thomas Magnum, in spite of his London-based manor.

Or he could be like PC Ernest 'Ernie' Trigg, (played by David Jason's brother, Arthur White) the police archivist in ITV1's *A Touch of Frost*. Although let's be honest, Stamp isn't that bright and would either get very, very bored or completely ruin the carefully designed records system. Whatever, he does, I hope Stamp is happy and maybe at last finds time for letting a spot of romance into his life.

And how about me? Looking back, I still think of myself as a leading man trapped in the wrong body. But I don't think I've done too badly at this acting lark. I've had over a 150 different roles during my career. Made countless TV appearances and played a popular character in one of TV's most successful shows for nearly a quarter of a century.

All I have ever wanted is to be a jobbing actor and I've always been up for a change so yes, going back out into the big wide world is daunting but it's also incredibly exciting. Of course I miss *The Bill* terribly. The people, Bosun House, being out on the streets every day, even wearing the uniform, despite it being so heavy and cumbersome. Being in civvies all the time is taking some getting used to, even now.

At least now I can do panto again and I'm relishing the chance to play some new characters in the coming years. Maybe being on the wrong side of the law for a change, playing a really nasty villain, that would be great fun. I hope I get invited onto TV quiz shows as I love doing stuff like *Countdown*. And most importantly, as well as providing for my family, I hope I can continue with my charity work as it really does mean so much to me. And how would I sum up my achievements? I hope I took my opportunities, given by great and supportive people I have met and worked with. Acting is in my very soul. I've been able to ply my craft and, thanks to *The Bill* be close to home and not always away on tour so I've been able to be home in the evenings to be a dad and a husband. To all who have and continue to support me, thank you, so, so much. And now on to the next chapter and.... who knows what?

# Acknowledgements

Reading my story back now that it is in book form, I am humbled and very aware of those who have touched my life and helped to mould the person contained in these pages. Having so many people to thank and so many involved in my life, is one of the reasons I decided to write this book.

There are a lot of people to thank so here goes...I miss my Mum and Dad a great deal and would like to thank them for their constant love and support and for their encouragement to have a go and try, which is the foundation that made me the man I am. And my sisters Pat and Jill for coming to shows and supporting all I did, giving me the down to earth 'he's just our brother' attitude, so vital to live this life on stage.

Thanks to my extended family for those parties; to Michael Coleman for phoning and keeping the family together; to my nephew Justin for the letters and now emails encouraging and giving unconditional support and love. Barrie Stacey, John Chilvers, Paul Dayson and Dick Tuckey who gave me my first breaks and allowed me to grow and experiment. And in Paul's case, for letting me, Cherry, and the babies live with him while employing me - now, that's way beyond friendship. Thanks also to numerous fellow performers, musicians, musical directors, directors, producers, writers, technicians and make-up and costume experts who make the magic happen.

I'm grateful to the team at *The Bill*, especially to Michael Chapman and Peter Cregeen, for giving me Tony Stamp; my fellow cast members, guest artistes, writers, producers, the wonderful crews and many friends gained from my time on *The Bill*.

Thanks to my beloved Cherry for always being there as my rock, my lover and my friend, giving unreserved love, support and constructive criticism in equal measure. I'll never be able to thank you enough. Matthew and Laura for making me so proud, feel so loved and so complete and, along with Cherry, for making those long hard days, those difficult decisions and painful times richer, more meaningful and totally worthwhile. Thank you from the bottom of my heart.

I'm grateful to the men and women of The Metropolitan Police, Commissioners Sir Peter Imbert, Sir John Stevens and Sir Ian Blair, British Transport Police Commissioner Ian Johnston and City of London Police Commissioner Mike Bowron. And to the officers I have spent hours with, asking questions, probing and annoying, I thank you for giving me the opportunity to watch first hand one of the most difficult professions in the world and to observe the joys, triumphs, frustrations and unrelenting service you give to others. You all helped me to create Tony Stamp.

I'm indebted to the staff and officers at Hendon, for those

hours of driver training, again giving me unique opportunities to gain expertise and feel so accepted at a driving institution which is the very envy of the world. The Police Federation of England and Wales, Joe Holness QPM and the National Police Memorial day; David French of the Police Dependents Trust; John Hussey and John Lancaster of the City of London Police Retired Officers and Widows Association.

I'm obliged to my brother Water Rats for the honour of being your King Rat for 2009. The Worshipful Company of Carmen, for all the history and joy of being a Liveryman, especially John and Marsha Rae Ratcliff. The many staff and volunteers from Scouting, National Holiday Fund, NSPCC, Childline, Variety Club and organisations who complete my life and give it purpose.

Thanks to my ghostwriter Nuala Giblin for making sense of my ramblings, deciphering my scrawl and for her patience, understanding and true professionalism along with a bit of encouragement. Thank you is just not enough. To Splendid Books' Steve Clark and Shoba Vazirani for your continued belief, encouragement, guidance and final production of this book which is so beyond all I expected.

I'm grateful to those people who have written to me in support, some for many years, the true fans who at time of writing still fill my mail bag each week, you are so special to me.

And finally to you the buyer or recipient of this book, I thank you, for choosing to share a few hours together with me. I hope you enjoy my book, my honest and humble account of what it is like to be Graham Cole.